Upside Down Evangelism

How Not to Manipulate People in a Post-Modern,
Post-Christian, Spiritually Alive Globalized World

Fábio Muniz

Hi Jacob,
I'm glad to be in touch with you!
May God guide you as you go to
college and make decisions in life.
May this book encourage and
inspire you. Take care!
Fábio
05/2018

Published by Underground Media
PO Box 75157
Tampa, FL 33675
tampaunderground.com
©2018 Underground Media

Design: Leann Theivagt
Photo: Martin Widenka

ISBN 978-1-9806169-7-9

Printed in the United States

What has been will be again, what has been done will be done again; there is nothing new under the sun.
Solomon (Ecclesiastes 1:9, NIV)

Contents

Foreword
Upside Down Evangelism

I love it whenever I encounter ideas and stories that reflect God's mission in culturally astute, spiritually sensitive, and intellectually original ways. Upside Down Evangelism is such a book; which doesn't surprise me, since it is written by a missionary practitioner who cares deeply about people and who desires passionately to see people encounter Jesus in life-changing ways. This combination in Fábio Muniz has resulted in an approach to evangelism that has the ring of authenticity to it.

God only knows that we need authentic approaches to sharing the good news with others. Too many formulas, 1-2-3's, and scripted conversations have passed for evangelism, and it is these that have given evangelism a bad rap. I share the author's disdain for such things. To abandon the practice of evangelism, however, is not the answer. The good news of Jesus is too good not to share with others. But how do we do it without impersonal formulas, worse, manipulative strategies? If this is an important question to you—and I hope it is—then this book is for you. True to its subtitle, it will show readers "how not to manipulate people in a post-modern, post-Christian, spiritually alive, globalized world."

Written in a highly personal style, Muniz discusses lessons learned and principles tested by his and his wife's encounters with people of several cultures, ages, and different professions, as they served as missionaries in Japan. He also appeals to theology and history grounding his thoughts about gospel communication in the Scriptures, even as he dabbles in cultural criticism to help shape an evangelism that befits the postmodern age.

I have the privilege of working alongside him and his wife Johnna in the global mission efforts of the Evangelical Covenant Church, and I am grateful for thinking practitioners like them. They not only have something to say to those outside the church, but they also have something to say to those inside the church—namely, how to love people with the gospel and how to share the greatest story ever told in a genuine way, while creating space for the Spirit, who alone can transform hearts and lives. I'm quite certain that the "upside down evangelism" you will encounter in this book will give you renewed hope in the practice.

On behalf of all those who long to be authentic in the communication of the gospel, thanks Fábio, for writing this book!

Al Tizon
Executive Minister of Serve Globally
Evangelical Covenant Church
Affiliate Professor of Missional and Global Leadership
North Park Theological Seminary

A Glimpse of my Existential Journey

Dear Reader,

Let me begin by saying that I have no intention of writing an extensive work here. There is nothing new under the sun (to be written or seen or heard) as Solomon wisely said. With that in mind, my primary goal is not to bring you a theological approach to missiology, but to describe an existential, sincere, and personal journey on the following pages.

I do not write from a Western point of view. Instead, I write from a world perspective with multicultural angles. This involves observing different cultures and peoples, civilizations of all eras, thousands of historical writings, and above all, with the understanding that God absolutely does not fit any religious package since no one has ever been able to scrutinize God or His mind. I love to see how scientific knowledge progresses, and it is wonderful to see the "divine tapestry" as scientists keep discovering multiple galaxies, measuring the dimension of our universe and invading the quantum sphere. I love watching documentaries, reading about the

Higgs boson, also called the God Particle, and other scientific findings that have been discovered by CERN, the European Organization for Nuclear Research.[1] And yet, God cannot be found in a scientific laboratory. God is not an object to be studied. However, He can be experienced when any human being at any moment, anywhere, seeks Him with honesty and sincerity. I do not consider myself a theologian, but simply a person who is passionate about the gospel, Jesus' teachings, and his historical life.

This is not an intellectual exercise, but a result of many hours of honest reflection, sincere devotion, meditation on the Scriptures, multiple questions, gratitude for hundreds of human encounters, a vulnerable heart to learn from several cultures and beautiful human beings. There is a deep necessity in the Christian world to see a practical, rather than just theoretical, lifestyle. Indeed, today what we need is to experience the powerful significance of giving life much more than our centenarian orthodoxy. The world is waiting for our authentic and real orthopraxy.

I started writing this document due to an email between my wife, Johnna, and her former missiology professor, Paul De Neui, from North Park Theological Seminary. She was asking him if he was going to be in Japan and if we could ask him some questions about what we were learning about missiology. In fact, as soon as I read their emails, most of these thoughts came to mind, and then, little by little, I unpacked them and put them into words chapter by chapter. On these pages, I will reveal a glimpse of thirty years in church and non-church environments—twenty years' experience as a tentmaker in Brazil, Canada, the United States, and Spain—and a fulfilled dream that took twenty years to realize.

After I left my job in the United States and came to Japan, I realized I could name this season in Japan one of the most exciting seasons of my life. A dream! In fact, working full time in ministry and having my wife and daughter be part of my mission journey has

---

[1] "Founded in 1954, the CERN laboratory sits astride the Franco-Swiss border near Geneva. The instruments used at CERN are purpose-built particle accelerators and detectors." For more about CERN, go to its official website, https://home.cern/.

brought my heart enormous joy and tremendous gratitude.

I feel as if I am writing a diary as part of my own missiological reflection and journey. Perhaps I will review these experiences in a few years from a different cultural perspective and different geography unknown to me at this time, but I do believe God has already planned new projects and mission for our family in the near future. My mother language is Portuguese, but I will pour out my heart and thoughts as best as I can to transmit these reflections to you in English.

Upside Down Evangelism: How Not to Manipulate People in a Post-Modern, Post-Christian, Spiritually Alive Globalized World will take you to some of my cross-cultural experiences in Brazil, Canada, Spain, the United States, and Japan. I am thankful to have connected with people of many different cultures, such as Latinos, Europeans, Americans, Canadians, Asians, many multi-ethnic people, among others these last two decades. I also want to highlight the fact that most of my thoughts have been inspired and influenced by the Brazilian pastor, Caio Fábio D'Araújo Filho. I am thankful for his influence in my life for more than twenty years. I have probably read around fifty of his more than one hundred books and had the privilege of traveling together with him to Israel in 1997. His main influences are authors and theologians Jacques Ellul,[2] C. S. Lewis,[3] and Søren Kierkegaard,[4] who have become inspiring sources for me as well.

---

[2] Jacques Ellul (1912–1994) was a French philosopher, sociologist, and lay theologian. A short biography is available on the International Jacques Ellul Society website, https://ellul.org/life/biography/.

[3] Clive Staples Lewis (1898–1963) was an Irish writer and one of the most influential writers of the 20th Century. C. S. Lewis's most popular book series, The Chronicles of Narnia, has sold over 100 million copies. You can read a fuller biography of him on his official website: http://www.cslewis.com/us/about-cs-lewis/. When I lived in Spain, I had the chance to go to Oxford and see most of the places related to his life, such as his home, church, gravesite, The Eagle and Child pub where he and J. R. R. Tolkien met to talk about their writings, etc. I also recommend the documentary *The Question of God: C. S. Lewis and Sigmund Freud*. It tells how Lewis came from a Protestant background, became an atheist,

With that, let's jump to the beginning of our journey. My purpose is to challenge you, the reader, to review and reflect on the deep but simple meaning of Missio Dei—God's mission—in the world and in your own life. I am not writing primarily to an audience of specialized scholars. Instead, I especially want to address this book to the following three audiences: 1) those who are thoughtful believers, perhaps attending a church but feeling stuck in a narrow definition of Evangelism - one that is a result of strategy and methodology. I hope these pages will revive God's role in your ministry as well as your practice of ministry, 2) those who are burned out on bad religion, 3) those who I meet nearly every week - my sincere friends who consider themselves atheist, agnostic, non-religious, spiritual or something else, who may not practice any religion, but are full of compassion and challenge me to be a better human being. May this book breathe new life into your perception of the world and its Creator.

With sincerity and transparency I hope to shake your worldview by defining the difference between Christianity as a religious phenomenon and the simplicity of following Jesus, the Eternal Christ of God. I want to encourage you to grow in knowledge and faith by learning how to rest in Him, the One who has called us to live our privileged journeys of proclaiming the Good News. We must be ever aware of the fact that it is never about us, but it is always about Him, and more than that, we must never forget that He is already working, in advance, all around the world in every single culture and human being.

but later found an authentic relationship with Jesus through the Gospels. In this documentary, a group of people (including a psychologist, a scientist, a Christian, an atheist, and an agnostic) take Lewis's and Freud's personal experiences and explore important philosophical and spiritual questions. This DVD is available on amazon.com.

[4] Encyclopedia Britannica identifies Søren Aabye Kierkegaard (1813–1855) as a "Danish philosopher, theologian, and cultural critic who was a major influence on existentialism and Protestant theology in the 20th Century." Find more on his life at https://www.britannica.com/biography/Soren-Kierkegaard

My special thanks to Serve Globally (formally Covenant World Mission) for allowing me to be part of its projects in the world. I'm grateful to Al Tizon for inviting me to his home, encouraging me to publish, and making time in his busy schedule to read my manuscript and write a foreword. Thanks to Johnna's aunt, Annette Hayward, who helped put this into book format.

I cannot forget our partner in ministry, Underground Network, who has made this project possible by doing the final editing and printing process. Thank you to everyone who has been part of my journey, some of whom will be remembered in the following pages. You have been instrumental in shaping my life through every talk, coffee chat, and encounter. Above all, I thank my dear wife, Johnna, for without her I would not be where I am right now in my existential journey, and you would not be able to have a clear English document without her initial edits.

Fábio Muniz
Starbucks Shonandai, Japan
March 10, 2017

Chapter 1

A Brief Background

Life can only be understood backwards; but it must be lived forwards.
Søren Kierkegaard

Between Life and Death: The Beginning of the Puzzle

When I look back on my life, I would not be able to make the pieces fit together even if I had planned this complex puzzle meticulously. Brazil has the largest Catholic population in the world,[5] and I grew up in a Catholic family in São Paulo. My family attended mass almost every Sunday. I attended First Communion classes and

---

[5] "There are an estimated 1.2 billion Roman Catholics in the world, according to Vatican figures. More than 40% of the world's Catholics live in Latin America. Brazil has the highest Catholic population of any country." You can read the full article "How many Roman Catholics are there in the world?" on the BBC website at http://www.bbc.com/news/world-21443313

studied my first eight years at a school that was managed by nuns. I remember that we as students, along with the teachers and nuns, did not go to our classrooms without praying together in the main entrance. During these early school years, my sister and I would frequently go to my aunt's house in the country to relax and be with our extended family. When I was four, however, I almost drowned in my aunt and uncle's swimming pool. When my cousin rescued me from the pool, I was unconscious. My aunt conducted CPR and I began breathing again. I will never forget that afternoon. Very often, even after all these years, I catch myself being grateful to be alive.

At age nine, I started attending a Presbyterian church. I went because I wanted to learn how to play guitar. I ended up spending almost ten years with that group of Presbyterians. After the first year at that church, I found out I had lost hearing in my left ear. One morning, I told my mom, "If I cover my right ear, I can't hear anything. But if I cover my left one, I can." No one could figure out how I lost 100 percent of hearing in my left ear. It was speculated that the cause was either my earlier near-drowning experience in the pool or an ear infection. I had been hoping to start drum classes, but was told I wouldn't be able to play them. However, this disadvantage would play a very important role in my life's formation by teaching me how to depend on God's grace as I studied business, worked for multinational companies, learned music, studied other languages, and preached the gospel.

Today I look back at those years and realize it was just the beginning of my journey. So, during the ten years after my Presbyterian experience, I got involved with various interdenominational and charismatic churches. In fact, as I write this paragraph, I am able to see an overlap of different denominations and several churches that molded me in my twenties and thirties. I was ordained a pastor by a nondenominational church at age twenty-four. By the time I turned thirty, I had been exposed to a variety of evangelical groups and theological thoughts. Lately, I've noticed that when I meet someone from any church or denomination for the first time, they often ask me about my background. The question is: "Fábio, how have you been formed spiritually? Please tell us your theological background."

I do not think my journey has a pattern because of several reasons. First, I believe God has a unique journey for each one of

His children. Second, I see that my journey is made up of unpredictable circumstances in which I was able to take advantage of places I lived, work environments, churches, cultures, and multiple groups of people I have been connected and exposed to. As I have been naturally living my life, God's pedagogical road has been built under my feet supernaturally. Maybe this hasn't been your path, but this has been my path. Your path is yours, mine is mine—it's as simple as that.

However, we have the same Father. Therefore, He is not just your Father, but mine too. He is not just my Father, but yours too! We find this when Jesus teaches us to pray, "Our Father in heaven, hallowed be your name."

My Formation and Personal Journey

When I was nineteen, I knew I had a call to ministry. I took a few classes in seminary, but quickly realized there was no time to actually practice ministry. I had to make a decision between theological studies and business. At that time, I decided to keep pursuing studies at the university to complete my business degree. As soon as I decided on a business education, I realized that classes like economy and communication, sociology and anthropology were invaluable to my ministerial formation. As I am one who loves reading broadly, my personal theological education started with studying the Bible meticulously and reading as many theological books as possible. In addition to that, for the last twenty years, I have been interested in many different subjects, from psychology to philosophy, science to history, politics to art, and these books helped round out my theological education. My studies and career ran parallel with ministry, making me a tentmaker for twenty years. My passion for languages, diverse cultures, business, and theology led me to study accounting, marketing, administration, and several languages in Brazil, Italy, Canada, Belgium, Spain, and Japan. I earned a degree in business in São Paulo, but also spent some time studying business English in Canada. When I was in Spain, I earned a master's in marketing at the University of Barcelona.

Back as a volunteer in my mid-twenties, I started a four-year stint of preaching and teaching a weekly Bible study and worship service in a Bolivian community in São Paulo. This experience became my first cross-cultural encounter, and I didn't even need to leave my hometown. Later in Canada, I had an opportunity to help with a church-planting project among Brazilians. I also got involved with Canadian and Jamaican churches in Toronto. While there, I realized I would not need to go anywhere to have a cross-cultural experience. More than a hundred forty languages are spoken daily in Toronto![6]

Dozens of cultures are represented in most of the neighborhoods. After Canada, and after spending almost forty days in the U.S. visiting friends, preaching, dreaming about the future, brainstorming, and talking about mission with missionaries and pastors, I ended up in Europe—in Barcelona, Spain—where I spent the next six years.

My European season was rich and full of intense experiences: working for multinational companies, working on my master's, getting involved with church planting projects with Covenant leaders, hosting small groups in my apartment, and developing language skills. I explored much of the continent, including its art, history, and geography, diving into the most intense period of my life.

My season in Europe made the subjects I had been reading come alive. They had been merely theory I had seen in books and articles until I went to Europe. While there for almost six years, as part of an intense learning process, I intentionally went to countless places where our Western thoughts were built and most of our Western history has been represented—from the Auschwitz concentration camp in Germany to the Louvre Museum in Paris; from Wittenberg to Geneva, and from Edinburgh to Zurich, where we have hundreds and hundreds of pages to remind us of the historical reformation

---

[6] The first time I learned that more than a hundred languages were spoken in Toronto was through a flyer given to me as I walked the streets of Toronto in 2004. On the official Toronto city hall website, you can read today that more than a hundred forty languages are spoken there. For more details about one of the most multicultural cities of the world, go to
http://www1.toronto.ca/wps/portal/contentonly?vgnextoid=dbe867b42d853410Vg nVCM10000071d60f89RCRD

spurred on by Luther, Melanchthon, Calvin, Knox, and Zwingli. And I went to more popular European art museums—to Reina Sofía, Prado, Picasso, and Dali in Spain; the National Gallery in London; Van Gogh's and Anne Frank's museums in Amsterdam; the homes of Freud and Mozart in Vienna, to the early Church footprints in Rome.

That tangible, in-person research helped form my theological reflection and take it to a different level of reality, shape, color, smell and form, one that stemmed from the real locations themselves. After traveling to several countries and experiencing a very intense period of studies and reflective moments, I met my wife, Johnna Hayward in Belgium. Her experience with a Congolese church in a French-speaking environment allowed me to add another cultural layer to this kaleidoscope and cultural portfolio. After a couple of years dating, we got married in Chicago and then moved to Florida.

After four years in Clearwater, we embraced a new project and lifestyle. We said yes to becoming short-term missionaries with Covenant World Mission/Serve Globally in Japan working with Brazilians, Latino-Japanese, Japanese, International groups, and an expressive group of Japanese people who have international tendencies speaking English, Portuguese, French and Spanish. As part of our project, our commitment was to support the Japanese Covenant denomination (NSKK) and its churches by preaching, teaching, playing concerts, and helping them with camping programs among other activities. In our last year in Florida, I was hired by a Brazilian Baptist church where I had already been preaching once a week for over a year as their associate pastor. At that moment, I realized it was the beginning of the end of my tentmaker season. As soon as we finished our fundraising race to come to Japan, I realized I started experiencing the end of the beginning of a new chapter in my life and ministry.

As a result of our partnership with Covenant World Mission/Serve Globally,[7] I started taking some credits from North

---

[7] Serve Globally (formerly Covenant World Mission) is the sending organization under the Evangelical Covenant Church, a multiethnic denomination in the United

Park Theological Seminary (NPTS) in Chicago, IL. As part of the process, in the next year or so, after an interview and theological paper, I hope to receive a ministerial license that is an American credential allowing me to apply for long-term projects. I also have a desire to take the spiritual direction course hosted by NPTS. However, for now, our plan is to finish Project Japan and be discerning about what God has prepared for our family, life and ministry for the next several years. There is a Portuguese saying, "A vida começa aos quarenta anos" that means, "life starts at forty." I'm forty-one and feel like I'm just starting life!

I am thankful for every experience I have accumulated so far, good and not so good, every single church, person, pastor, denomination I have had an opportunity to meet and work with, for every single city and country I have visited, every possibility to improve a language I have studied so far, and every culture I have been learning about. With that in mind, I want to let you know that these past experiences have helped me develop some partial conclusions I will begin to explain here. By the way, I call them partial because I would like to make our brother Paul's words my own: "Now I know only in part; then one day I will know fully, even as I have been fully known" (1 Corinthians 13:12b).

States and Canada with ministries on five continents. Founded in 1885 by Swedish immigrants, see more at http://www.covchurch.org/what-we-do/serve-globally/.

Chapter 2

A Quick Word To Kick Off

"Much of Christian history has manifested a very different god than the one Jesus revealed and represented."
Richard Rohr

For Those Who Struggle with Religion (like me)

This is not new. As I started my preface by quoting Solomon, "there is nothing new under the sun", and as in the quote above by Richard Rohr,[8] much of Christianity as a religious movement has shown a very different god than Jesus announced, proclaimed and taught. Without understanding this difference, we will not get very far. Why is it so important to comprehend this? Why do we find so many people, especially young adults, with an enormous resistance to talk

---

[8] Throughout this book, I will be quoting different people. Just because I quote something they say does not mean I agree with everything they write, say or represent. My filter, my hermeneutic key, is Jesus, so all that aligns with the Person of Jesus and his teachings is truth because He is the Truth.

about God, religion and faith? Have you ever met friends who have a strong reaction, like a "chronic allergy," when the topic is Jesus? What made generation after generation create individuals who respond to any Christian talk with deep disappointment and signs of anger? How can we define post-christian cultures, post-christian continents and countries? Have you ever thought of cultures, continents and countries that have little to no Christian influence?

I would like to start this chapter by telling you that every believer in Jesus would have a much better understanding of what I am talking about if they read the book *The Subversion of Christianity*[9] by French philosopher, writer and theologian, Jacques Ellul. It is the most accurate and detailed work regarding Christianity as a political, anthropological, social, economical and religious phenomenon. It is absolutely essential to cut the religious "umbilical cord" in order to put all people, believers and those who do not profess Christ, on the same level, dismantling the supremacy that has sometimes been associated with Christianity for hundreds and hundreds of years. This supremacy is seen when Christians act as if they possess certain knowledge that most of the world does not have. As a result of this perceived special knowledge, generations of people who see themselves outside of Christianity have built walls and responded to anything related to Jesus with a severe repugnancy. I do not want to be misunderstood. As you keep traveling step by step on this road that I am building here, you will realize the difference between being a follower of Christianity and a follower of Christ, being a Christian

---

[9] Translated from the French edition *La subversion du Christianisme,* copyright Éditions du Seuil, Janvier 1984. If you are interested in reading Jacques Ellul's book, you can order it on https://www.amazon.com. A description taken from amazon.com: "Pointing to the many contradictions between the Bible and the practice of the church, Jacques Ellul asserts in this provocative and stimulating book that what we today call Christianity is actually far removed from the revelation of God. Successive generations have reinterpreted Scripture and modeled it after their own cultures, thus moving society further from the truth of the original gospel. The church also perverted the gospel message, for instead of simply doing away with pagan practice and belief, it reconstituted the sacred, set up its own religious forms, and thus resacralized the world."

as the product of a religious label, the sub-product of a religious membership, and a Christian as a disciple of Jesus, the Eternal Christ of God.

Jesus never asked his disciples to teach moral laws and impose a group of rules. Jesus never taught that his disciples would be better or superior than everybody else. In reality, his disciples were supposed to be like Him - loving the poor, working for justice, walking with marginalized individuals who were rejected and discriminated by religious groups and society, embracing the foreigner and the immigrant cause, visiting the prisoner, having mercy and compassion for those who felt weak and sick, meeting human needs, giving bread to the hungry, water to the thirsty, clothing the naked, practicing forgiveness and generosity, being a peacemaker and being present to the orphan and widow. It is how the world will know we are disciples of Jesus, not by words, but by an authentic action immersed in love - not through our orthodoxy, but through our orthopraxis. By this everyone will know that you are my disciples, if you love one another (John 13:35).

The only dogma the disciples of Jesus were given was the dogma of love. Our orthodoxy has no power if there is not love. Our catechism has no importance if there is not love. Our credentials and religious titles are meaningless if there is not love. The apostle Paul wrote, "If I speak in the tongues of men or of angels, but do not have love, I am only a resounding gong or a clanging cymbal. If I have the gift of prophecy and can fathom all mysteries and all knowledge, and if I have faith that can move mountains, but do not have love, I am nothing. If I give all I possess to the poor and give over my body to hardship that I may boast, but do not have love, I gain nothing" (1 Corinthians 13:1-3). Our primary call as disciples of Jesus is to find life-giving ways of living for all people, for God's glory and my neighbors' good, bearing fruits of love and justice. For it is by our fruits we will be known - it is our active faith in love. "For in Christ Jesus neither circumcision nor uncircumcision has any value. The only thing that counts is faith expressing itself through love" (Galatians 5:6).

For Those Who Think There's Something Wrong with Christianity

Most people I've met these last several years who might not consider themselves Christians know chapters of historical Christianity better than most of my church friends. I am not surprised when I see my church friends having trouble connecting to people outside of our church walls. I am not surprised when I see less and less pastors and church leaders having meaningful, intentional interactions with perceived non-Christians. What is wrong with us? Why have we constructed apartheids for centuries on behalf of God or on behalf of our high moral standard? Why don't most of those who claim to be disciples of Jesus hang out with those who do not attend their church? How could we be so different than Jesus? Do we think when Jesus hung out with tax collectors, prostitutes and sinners, as they got together, they all said "Hosanna, blessed is he who comes in the name of the Lord?' Don't you think they might have sworn and said vulgar things as they had dinner together?

How do I react to my friends who don't consider themselves to be Christians? Am I able to have a cup of coffee and talk about life, family, listen to them, their hobbies and be interested in their journey? Do I always try to convince them to come to church? Do I always present a certain side of me that directly or indirectly tries to tell them that I know God and they do not? Please, be honest today and ask yourself how many non-church-going friends you have. How many of your church friends have friends that don't go to church? How many friends do your pastors and the leaders of your church have that don't go to church?

Unfortunately, Richard Rohr[10] is right when he says, "Much of Christian history has manifested a very different god than the one Jesus revealed and represented." A few months ago Johnna and I played in a concert at an evangelistic event in a certain area of Japan. At the end of our concert, we came to the organizer and said: "We are more than glad to come here, but we thought this would be an event for people who don't usually come to church, where were

---

[10]See more about Richard Rohr at https://cac.org/richard-rohr/richard-rohr-ofm/.

they?" They were not there! We could not believe it when we asked how many friends this small group of people had that didn't go to church. Immediately, their silence was our answer. When we left, we went back to our car a bit sad, and Johnna said to me, "Fábio, our experience in Japan has basically been speaking to church people on the weekends and hanging out with non-church people all the other days."

Johnna was right. I immediately started thinking about and asking myself why most Christians have lost the ability to build connections with non-Christians. Our call is definitely not to establish "ghettos" and build walls. Our call is to be salt and light in the world - it is easy to be salt in the saltcellar. It is easy to say "Amen" in our churches. It is easy to be next to individuals who think like us. By the way, in certain places, it seems to me I am in a clone factory - they all speak like their pastor, they all dress like their pastor, they all greet each other in the same fashion, they have lost their individuality and absorbed a specific church-denomination culture. This is the risk, result and dangerous path of being salt in the saltcellar. On the other hand, the disciples of Jesus are supposed to be salt in an insipid and bland society. The disciples of Jesus are supposed to be spread out in the world - outside of our saltcellar. Therefore, our churches, gatherings and prayer meetings are made to be "pit stops" where we change our tires, put gasoline in our tanks, check our brake pads and then, back to the race, back to the world!

After Jesus' resurrection, do you think the disciples stayed in Jerusalem for the rest of their lives? The disciples stayed together only for a few years after Jesus' death. According to Christian tradition, Thomas went to Syria and India, Philip went to Carthage in North Africa, Mathew went to Persia and Ethiopia, Bartholomew went to India with Thomas and then Ethiopia, Southern Arabia and Greater Armenia, and Peter and Paul died in Rome under the Emperor Nero. They were all martyred except John, who died a natural death from old age. However, John was exiled to the island of Patmos after escaping unharmed being thrown into boiling oil during Domitian's persecution in Rome. Perhaps persecution was "necessary" to make them assume their call to the Great Commission and go to different parts of the continent in order to spread the good news of Jesus.

Our call to the world is to show our identity through our eyes as disciples of Jesus - our passion and action, energy and breath, enthusiasm and daily giving of our lives should be sensed by, and reflected to, everyone who crosses our path. More than that, you and I are called to get into dark places and shine as lights of the world, embracing individuals whom no one wants to embrace, listening to those whom no one wants to listen to, loving those whom no one wants to love. Our call is not to walk through this existence carrying a certain supremacy over everybody else, but as we walk on the road of life, we are to humbly proclaim that God was in Christ, reconciling the world to himself, no longer counting people's sins against them (2 Corinthians 5:19).

At this point, I invite you to think of your family members and backgrounds. Do a quick exercise and also look at your friends' experiences. Observe and try to figure out their own Christian/religious experiences. If you find it difficult to do this exercise, go back and open any historical book on Christianity as a religious phenomenon over hundreds and hundreds of years, including its powerful and negative influence. You will probably find people who have been hurt by Christianity as a religion. Unfortunately, this is the testimony for many of us. Unfortunately, this is the background of many of the people I have met these last ten years. I think I am not the only one meeting people who have been hurt by Christianity as a religion and churches as political institutions. Do you also have this experience?

Being a disciple of Jesus means to have an awareness of who God is and how we should develop as human beings. We grow in comprehension, maturity and understanding by observing how Jesus lived his own life. We are able to understand and discern, learn and comprehend how to become better fathers, better neighbors, better wives, better sons, better business men, better pastors. By now, as you probably already realized, I have been dissociating, disconnecting, separating Christianity as a religious-institutional-historical movement from Jesus, the historical Christ that is presented to us through the Gospels. You may ask me: Fábio, why do you think this disassociation is essential when we talk about missiology? Do you think it is really important to make this difference? Do you believe people who are not familiar with our church environment would understand what you are talking about?

Are Jesus and Christianity the Same?

There are a lot of Jesus' teachings in the movement called Christianity, but Christianity is not 100% equal to Jesus. The word "Christianity" and how Jesus lived are not synonymous. They are not! I am sorry if I am shocking you, but God is not equal to Christianity. God is spirit. God is much bigger than Christianity. God is God. I cannot define and see Him only through Christian lenses and then relativize Him through Christian categories. With nearly every person I meet, I work through these basic steps in order to put him or her face to face with the historical Jesus in the Gospel narratives. These last fifteen years, having met countless individuals in South America, Europe, North America and currently in Japan, I have been taking time to remove Jesus from any religious package, including Christianity, in order to have an opportunity to present Jesus in his true form, without any religious baggage.

Look around you. Look at the universe. According to science developed with the use of the Hubble telescope, we have an estimated 100 billion galaxies in the universe[11] and our Milky Way galaxy alone has up to 400 billion stars.[12] Think of millions of stars and how some of them are dying somewhere right now and think of how many asteroids are collapsing right now somewhere in the universe. Look at the unbelievable beauty around you. Think of the mountains, islands, and forests. Thousands of rivers everywhere. Imagine the immense ocean and the millions and millions of creatures that live there - some we have never seen, some we do not even know exist.

How could we try to define God? How could we confine, label and patent Him in any religious box? We definitely would be foolish and pathetic if we tried to make God fit to any of our many human systematic theological thoughts and debates. As a result of an immense divorce and deep disassociation from what Christians have said on behalf of God and how Christians have lived out their faith

---

[11] https://www.space.com/25303-how-many-galaxies-are-in-the-universe.html
[12] https://www.universetoday.com/102630/how-many-stars-are-there-in-the-universe/

for centuries, this discrepancy has undoubtedly constructed a time bomb and post-Christian society. Our current generation is not able to separate the Jesus presented in the Gospels from the Jesus of Christianity. Regrettably, it seems that for most people on the planet, Christianity and Christ are the same. What has been the result of this discrepancy? How can I talk about Jesus to someone who is from Buddhist/Shinto Japan or Buddhist/Hindu Sri Lanka? How can I share my personal experience in a society that has a tired, skeptical, post-Christian environment like Europe? How can I make any approach about faith in the Americas (South, North or Latin) where people are bombarded by religious talks all the time? Actually, when I take Jesus out of all religious packages and encourage individuals to reflect on historical facts, observe spiritual leaders throughout history, and compare them to the historical Jesus and his teachings, we are able to go deeper and discuss spirituality and faith. With that beginning, we often easily begin to find what I define as common ground. Of course, most of the time, the way it unfolds depends on the person with whom I'm interacting. We might end our talk by mentioning an atheist or agnostic philosopher who had negative experiences with religion. For example, the Dutch philosopher, Spinoza, who came from a religious Jewish background, or the German Nietzsche who came from a Protestant background, or many others.

Very often, our conversations touch on current or past historical events related to Christianity as a political-religious phenomenon or any other religion as a result of human construction. No matter what, as soon as common ground is established, we agree on historical events, backgrounds and experiences of thinkers, differences between cultures, etc. After that, we may begin sharing our own personal experiences, building a friendship by becoming more open and vulnerable with each other, sharing our views of the world, general human traumas, and then, without realizing it, we start having a glimpse, a smooth conversation about Jesus, his teachings and his historical life.

Today in our globalized world, it almost doesn't matter what the other person's background is. When I meet someone and talk about the historical Jesus, I can almost always follow the same steps in each conversation. However, I take into account where we are geographically, the present culture in which we are, and some external features such as political and historical events that will easily build connection. As soon as we detect a globally minded person in any cosmopolitan city in the world, we should be aware of the fact that they belong to a unique category and group of people. Globally minded people are often the type of people with whom it is easiest and fastest to start a conversation, find common ground and build a possible friendship. This reality has been spreading to almost every location with almost all human beings. The world has become small.

An Introduction to our Global World - For Pastors and Missionaries

As you know, we do not need to go to China to be exposed to Chinese culture, or to India to have a taste of Indian culture, or to any other place to meet a specific culture due to what we have named as globalization. In my Canadian seasons (one in 2000 and the other 2004-2005), I was amazed to see the number of languages, diverse nationalities and different cultures in just one place, one city, or even one neighborhood. While globalization has had many wonderful effects, it is interesting to see how the whole process has affected our missiological approaches. It is undeniable how language skills play a very important role in the global world scenery. We will go deeper into this later, but for now, let me give you a glimpse of what I am talking about. In Barcelona ten years ago, I remember a conversation I had in Spanish with a woman from Germany:

"How do you speak Spanish so well?" I asked her with surprise.

"Well, you also speak Spanish very well," she responded.

"The difference is that Spanish is very similar to Portuguese, but German and Spanish?!" I said, smiling. "I am not surprised you speak English well because of the similarities between English and German, but Spanish? I'm very impressed," I completed.

In Europe, I found a very high number of people speaking more than three different languages. It was not rare to find a Bulgarian or Finnish person speaking Spanish, a Polish person speaking French and Russian, a Peruvian speaking Italian or French, or a Swiss person speaking three or more languages. After my six years in a European context, I could see the power of language skills in a world that has almost "lost its walls" due to the globalization phenomenon. It is definitely an amazing privilege to use languages to build common ground as a tool in our mission life. Recently, my Spanish conversation with a Japanese student at Starbucks in Chigasaki almost became a therapy session as she shared her struggles at work and the depression she was feeling.

Johnna and I have been speaking to Japanese people and connecting to them in English, Spanish, Portuguese and French. My experiences in Japan with globally minded people have been somehow even more pedagogical than those I had during my European, North and South America seasons. One of the reasons for this is something we have found incredible - the fact that Japanese people who have international tendencies become more open to talk to us about faith, spirituality and even their personal struggles than what would be usual for Japanese people because of their global exposure. Indeed, it is very uncommon to find people in Japanese culture (those who have not traveled internationally) who are willing to openly speak to others about supposed taboo subjects such as family, personal traumas, religion, Jesus, suicide attempts in their families, or even to ask for someone's help or advice.

This is completely different from most Latin American and African countries where people meet you today and the next day you are already having a barbecue, watching soccer and drinking beer. Those are known as warmer or hot cultures. Some European countries are more similar to Japan in some characteristics and they are known as cold cultures.[13] But take a Japanese person who has learned a foreign language, and suddenly, they no longer look or act like a Japanese person. In other words, their self-protection and resistance go away and they become much more vulnerable, friendly and open to listen to our experiences and faith.

Since I am bringing up my experience in Japan speaking foreign languages, perhaps you are wondering, "Aren't you supposed to learn the language of the country in which you are immersed?" The answer is yes, yes and yes. It is crucial and essential to speak the

---

[13] *Foreign to Familiar: A Guide to Understanding Hot - And Cold - Climate Cultures* by Sarah A. Lanier.

language of their hearts. If you are in Spain, please learn Spanish. If you are in Brazil, please study Portuguese. If you are in China, please study Mandarin. If you are in Japan, please study Japanese! I have trouble understanding some Brazilians and Spanish-speakers who go to Miami or Los Angeles and try to plant churches and work only with the Brazilian and Latino communities. They spend years and years in those places and yet are not able to communicate in English at all. I am still talking about my Brazilian and Latino friends to whom I would say: "Please, do not go to Europe if you are not able to speak at least one or two of the following languages: English, French, or Italian, in addition to your Spanish and Portuguese. Please, stay where you are and make your own culture and country your mission field. Stay where you are and make your work environment your mission field, but do not go to a different country to work only with your culture and people."

I have seen this scenery dozens of times. The result is that pastors and missionaries get burned out. Their children are speaking the language of the country. Parents cannot understand their own children. Countless family conflicts take place as the parents become bitter and wish they could go back to their home country: Brazil, Argentina, Peru or wherever they are from. Their children often do not know anything about their parent's original countries and want to stay where they were born or have been growing up.

I cannot condone American (or British, Australian, any English-speaking) pastors who lead international churches and do not attempt at all to speak the language of the country. Although they are in an English-speaking environment, I am discouraged by the fact that they are not even able to have a shallow and short conversation in Spanish, French or Japanese with a neighbor, at the train station or grocery store. It is not just disrespectful, but to any native speaker's perception, they are transmitting a lack of interest regarding the culture in which they are immersed.

A few months ago, Johnna and I got together with a Japanese youth pastor. Her church also has Portuguese and Spanish services to reach out to the numerous Brazilian-Japanese and Latino-Japanese people in our neighborhood. She said: "I want to understand why some Japanese people, who love languages and come to our services to speak a foreign language like Spanish say yes to accept Jesus, they say yes to receive our prayers, and then they never come back to our church after their first very "positive experience." Johnna wisely responded: "Japanese people are not supposed to say no." I am sure my French friends would not have any difficulty saying a direct "no, thank you" if they had the same experience in church and were asked for prayers and commitments. The fact is that Japanese people are basically taught not to refuse anything. "No" is not part of their culture. It is not even part of Japanese daily vocabulary.

Therefore, when Japanese people do not want to accept your invitation to do something or go somewhere, one of the ways they have to say it is "chotto…" that would be translated in this context something like "well, that's a little…" and they don't even need to finish the sentence. It is already understood that they can't do it. As we see, it is not only language that makes a difference but how that language is contextualized in a given culture. It is the powerful combination of a foreign language, without the pressure that sometimes comes from a church environment, that make an extremely and complex culture like Japanese culture more open to listen to stories about the historical Jesus. This is especially true when one is able to deconstruct a sophism and concept that Jesus is just one more invasive and Western religion heritage. What our churches, not just in Japan, but all around the world should understand is that our neighbors, friends, colleagues and families do not necessarily need to come to our churches (read churches as buildings) to accept Jesus - We are the Church.

How Do You Define Church?

Very often we transfer our responsibility of being agents of God's grace to our pastor's message on Sunday in order to try to convert our husband, daughter, colleagues or neighbors, instead of being the living message to each one of them. Very often we transfer our responsibility to a couple's retreat event, a gospel concert, etc. There is nothing wrong with those events, but the responsibility is mine. It is yours. At this point, we may ask ourselves the meaning of being the Church. What is the nature of the Church? What is our call? Are we supposed to bring everyone to our buildings? Is there any special force in our temples? We probably forget that Church is not a human institution or organization, it is not buildings or hierarchical structures, gothic or baroque architectures. Jesus did not have a cathedral and a big cross on the top of a roof in his mind when He talked about Church. "And I also say to you that you are Peter, and on this rock I will build My church, and the gates of Hades shall not prevail against it" (Matthew 16:18).

In fact, there is nothing special inherently coming from our pulpits, no divine energy from a piece of wood or stone. God is not limited to any geography, building or certain square meter. God is in our churches because we are there - we are His Church. God is in me. God is in you. God is in us, therefore, wherever we get together, in His name, He will be there. Some individuals may think that God may punish them if the service starts at 6pm and they get to the temple at 6:15pm. I remember such reverence when I was a child in our Presbyterian church. For some individuals, they believe God may not hear their prayers unless they pray in those "sacred square meters."

To the contrary, Church is an organic, dynamic and living organism. Church is a communion of fellowship of believers. "There is neither Jew nor Gentile, neither slave nor free, nor is there male and female, for you are all one in Christ Jesus" (Galatians 3:28). It is not a club or an aggregation of individuals. Church is *ekklesia*, a Greek noun that means "to call together" or "to call into assembly."[14] It is no coincidence that Luther fought against the Christian institution represented by the Catholic Church by saying "Christians should sign their names and meet alone in a house somewhere to pray, to read, to baptize, to receive the sacrament, and do other Christian works."[15] Jesus said, " For where two or three are gathered together in My name, I am there in the midst of them" (Matthew 18:20). We are the Church when we get together anywhere with sincerity and honesty in the name of Jesus - at a public plaza, bar, hotel or under a tree. We may go and attend a church, building, or temple and have the risk of not living as Church. This happens when we lose the meaning of being Church due to our political-hierarchical-selfish-human interests.

---

[14] http://www.biblestudytools.com/lexicons/greek/nas/ekklesia.html

[15] p. 102, *Living Faith*, by the Faculty of North Park Theological Seminary.

"Priesthood of all believers" was one of the main phrases in the Reformation. The Reformers tried to release the Church from the power of the clergy. It is not a coincidence that Calvin encouraged everyone to be his or her own priest, not needing a mediator, pastor, pontiff or anyone else to connect with God. Jesus is the only mediator between humans and God. "For there is one God and one Mediator between God and men, the man Christ Jesus," (1 Timothy 2:5). We are all called to be the people that Peter wrote about, "But you are a chosen generation, a royal priesthood, a holy nation, His own special people, that you may proclaim the praises of Him who called you out of darkness into His marvelous light" (1 Peter 2:9). Therefore, everyone is supposed to be a minister and everyone, including pastors and church leaders, can be ministered to.

Although every disciple of Jesus is called to be a minister, Church has individuals who have been called to a special function in this organic, dynamic and living organism. However, those credentials and certificates, masters in divinity and missiology do not give them superior status. Based on this, we see the church is a training center or pit stop and we can remind ourselves that our mission field is outside of our church walls. Let's go to the next chapter. I would like to talk about this topic a little bit more.

Chapter 3

Make Your Life Your Mission and Your Mission Your Life[16]

"I look upon all the world as my parish."
John Wesley

No Copyright Needed! Preach This Message For Free

I grew up in a small church in São Paulo, Brazil. I heard about evangelism and missions often. I still remember I was only nine or ten years old when I saw missionaries preaching and talking about missions in my local church for the first time. They talked about Africa, native Brazilians, how to translate the Bible into their

---

[16] I preached this sermon for the first time in 2007 in La Coruña, Spain. Since then, I have been developing different versions and preaching the same sermon in different cities and countries. Although I have adjusted my message according to the cultural context in which I preach, the core message is the same: Make your life your mission and your mission your life.

languages, the poor conditions of many peoples and tribes and their struggles to live life. They shared how to reach out to the Middle East and countries in Asia like Japan and China. Those places were really far away from me and the description explained by the missionaries was even more far away from my own reality as a student. They were not wrong, but I found out later that missions and evangelism were not just for some specific group of people, pastors who had credentials, or missionaries who were sent by a Christian organization or a local church.

The Great Commission is well known: "Therefore go and make disciples of all nations, baptizing them in the name of the Father and of the Son and of the Holy Spirit, and teaching them to obey everything I have commanded you. And surely I am with you always, to the very end of the age" (Matthew 28:20). In our translations, both of the verbs "go" and "make" are imperative. Nevertheless, the only imperative verb in Greek (the original text) is "make" disciples because "go" is supposed to be translated as "going." It means *as you go on your way* or *when/while you are going*, make disciples.[17] There is a powerful significance when you understand the meaning of this call and you become aware of the fact that there is constant movement in the form of this verb. The sense is: Wherever you go and wherever you are, make disciples.

A couple of years ago, one of our church partners asked me how long I had been a missionary. I thought, "It depends on what you want to hear." I could answer that I've been a missionary since I was nineteen years old, or I could say that this is my first time to become a missionary. The other question was, "How long have you been in full-time ministry?" Again, it depends. I have been in full-time ministry since I was nineteen, but I was bi-vocational. I worked a job, but also preached in different places, worked with families and young adults, visited and counseled people. Coming to Japan was my first time to work "full-time" in ministry and depend on people's generosity as most people think of it.

Have you ever caught yourself thinking "I wish I could be in

---

[17] https://churchhealthwiki.wordpress.com/2017/05/08/great-commission-how-its-4-verbs-tell-us-our-purpose/

ministry full-time" or "I wish I could have a cross-cultural experience and embrace a mission project" or even "I wish I could have a function in my local church"? Look around and see your questions from a different perspective. I had my first cross-cultural experience in São Paulo preaching in Spanish to Bolivians for four years. And as I mentioned about Canada, more than one hundred languages are spoken on the streets of Toronto. Japanese people are definitely able to have a cross-cultural and missional experience in Tokyo! I have good news for you. You are a missionary! You are in ministry full-time and you live in a constant mission field!

Often, I hear people saying, "I wish I could serve Jesus freely and quit my job." We have 7 billion opportunities to show God's love and serve Jesus by serving and loving our neighbors because we currently have 7 billion people in the world! Make your life your mission and your mission your life. Make your home your first mission field. Make your work environment your mission field. If you go to Starbucks or any grocery store, make those places your mission field. A student might make his university his mission field. A nurse or doctor might make their hospital their mission field. A minister or pastor might try to conquer the entire world for Christ and neglect and forget to spend time with her daughter. A Christian businessman might use every single meeting in his agenda for God's glory, but forget to book a date during the week with his wife. Your ministry is your family. Your ministry is your wife and daughter, your son and your husband. They are more important than our pulpits, agenda and meetings. Make your city your mission field. Make Tokyo your mission field. Make Chicago your mission field. Make Rio de Janeiro your mission field. Make any train station your mission field. Make every single place you go your mission field because you are "going," you are "on your way." Starbucks, airports, parks, your school and your work environment are your parish!

A few months ago I was asked how we could connect to so many different people. Which techniques did we use to make our approach? How did we know when to finish talking about the weather, our job or any other "secular" topic and start a "sacred" conversation talking about Jesus and church stuff? Well, my answer was a simple "I do not know." I do not make this split and division in my mind. The only thing that I know for sure is we are honest when we connect to any person. We do not expect any result from our meetings or conversations. We do not meet a neighbor and say "hi" expecting him to come to our church next Sunday. I do not talk to a Starbucks staff member expecting him or her to pray in a few months with me, "Lord Jesus, come into my heart." It could happen, and would be amazing if it did, but that is not my first goal. The main goal is to get together and be close to people for who they are. We are just ready to listen to them. We ask honest questions. We develop sincere friendships.

Everything comes together. Everything is mixed and integrated together. There is a well-known quote attributed to Saint Francis who alluded to this way of life when he said, "Preach the Gospel at all times and when necessary, use words!"[18] This doesn't mean words aren't important. It means our actions should preach the Gospel so loudly that we only need to use words when they will enhance our actions, rather than take away from them. I recently heard a Brazilian pastor preaching and I liked what he said about this topic. When someone is saying one thing and doing another, people say, "Your life is talking so loud I cannot hear what you are telling me!"

It amazes me to see how Jesus naturally went from one place to another, how he was always out and about living life, participating in weddings, visiting people, going to synagogues, talking to everyone. It amazes me to see how he treated women, sinners, tax collectors and how he challenged religious people to live out their beliefs and leave their hypocrisy and false spirituality. No methodologies. No formulas. No human constructions. He just lived life and met people's needs as he went on his way forgiving their sins, healing their diseases, receiving and embracing marginalized people.

---

[18] For years I have heard and read that Saint Francis said, "Preach the Gospel at all times and when necessary, use words!" As far as we know, he never actually said it. However, it does not diminish the significant truth that this statement carries by itself. Therefore, your life and words are supposed to walk together because your attitude shows who you are. You can read more about it on https://focusoncampus.org/content/did-francis-really-say-preach-the-gospel-at-all-times-and-if-necessary-use-words.

Make your life your mission and your mission your life. Divine appointments will take place as you live life. As you go on your way… We might see what we call results in life. We might not. But, it is said that evangelism is to bring one person one step closer to Christ. Therefore, as you and I live our lives naturally, the supernatural power of God will come over our daily activities, our daily routine, and we will be able to be His witnesses wherever we go. May God help us to live life as we see Him going before us and actively working in cultures, people's hearts and divine circumstances and appointments.

Chapter 4

Any Conversation May be a Divine Appointment

"Now he had to go through Samaria."
John 4:4

When Extraordinary Invades Ordinary

If I met the apostle John today, I would say "John, you were not right. Jesus did not have to go through Samaria! Did you not know it was dangerous? Did you not know Samaritans and Jews did not get along? Did you not know there were different cultural, political and religious points of view between them? Did you not know a man and woman alone would not give anyone a good impression? Yes, he did know this! As the text goes on, we understand why John said that Jesus had to go through Samaria. My Portuguese Bible version says "Era necessário passar por Samaria" that means it was necessary to go through Samaria. I like that. It was necessary, but not really…

In 2002, I applied for a management position to work for a multinational Swiss company in Brazil. By the time I applied for that position, I was already working and doing ministry in tandem even though I had no idea what it meant to be a tentmaker. The fact is that as soon as I saw the pictures of the company on the walls and all the places they had branches, I immediately thought, "This company could be my door to becoming a missionary outside of Brazil if I could work for them in other locations."

From now on, the names you read are not the real ones due to privacy. Ricardo interviewed me for a branch manager position. After a few weeks, the company hired me and Ricardo was my boss for a couple of years. When I left the company and went to Canada, Ricardo and I stayed in touch via Messenger. His marriage broke up, and after a deep personal crisis, he gave his life to Jesus. When I passed through Brazil before moving to Europe, I could not believe it, but we went to a Baptist church in São Paulo and sat next to each other, participating in the entire service together. During that short visit to Brazil, between Canada and Spain, he invited me to preach to his family in a home group meeting. Ricardo and I have kept in touch via Facebook. Last year, before I came to Japan, we got together for coffee and talked about our personal journeys with Jesus. In 2002 when he hired me to work for the company in Brazil, I could never have guessed that more than a decade after my very first interview, I would be having coffee with him as my brother in Christ. As I think of him and write this, I am able to see one of the first divine appointments that undeniably took place in my life.

It would take a long time to relay all the details, but the truth is that in 2005 I became a branch manager for the same company in Barcelona, Spain. For six years, I experienced the richest existential, cultural and most pedagogical season of my life. In addition, I met the one who became my wife, Johnna, in Belgium during that important and unique European season. It was necessary. He had to go through...

Divine appointments take place constantly in our day-to-day routine. Are you sensitive to see divine appointments when they take place in your life? Are you able to discern a friendship, talk, or unexpected meeting that could change somebody else's life? Are you the type of person who thinks, "I have to bring someone to my church" (read church as building)? "I have to plant a church as part of my missiological project, or I won't see the fruit?" Or do you ever think, "If I just pass by someone's life, who is going to intentionally follow up and take care of him or her when I go somewhere else?"

In the past, most missionaries were expected to plant a church. It was inconceivable to think about mission without connecting it to church planting. This reality has changed a little, but I still often hear questions about my journey as I talk to pastors and missionaries. The truth is, everyone has a different call and we are all called to be agents of grace. I participated in two church planting projects - one in Mississauga, Canada and the other one in Barcelona, Spain. I was a pioneer in Brazil by opening a conventicle (small group) preaching to the Bolivians for four years. It started in 2000 when a number of Bolivians came to São Paulo. The Korean community took advantage of the situation, providing them very minimal resources such as housing and opportunities for low-wage employment in the clothing industry. During that time, I preached to the Bolivian community with the permission of the Korean owners. Over time, the Bolivian community gained a little more stability, their own houses and their own factories making clothes, still for the Korean owners. At that time, they had more freedom to have a Sunday service, so we began that together. I had the chance to baptize people and the church grew very easily through friendship and connection. Some even asked me to provide names for their children. A friend of mine took care of the group when I left for Canada. Then, eventually, a Bolivian pastor who grew up in the community continued the church, renting a venue, and weekly services still continue today.

My call is not to be a pastor of a local church even though I pastor people weekly. My call is not to plant a church even though I am planting seeds in people's hearts weekly. In short, as I have passed by hundreds of people in different cities and continents, I've been able to follow up with some of them, however, many of them, have only been in my life for a season or a certain purpose. For me, planting a church can be the natural and spontaneous by-product of investing in friendships and community and is not dependent on a building or structure.

For Those Who Believe There is More Than What We Can See

It was some time between 2005 and 2006. I used to go to the beach in Barcelona around ten o'clock at night. Sometimes I broke my routine and went to the beach even later. I love to spend time with people, I am a people person, but I also love to be alone and have my private time. Johnna knows it better than anybody else. Well, that night, I took some time to pray, be quiet, think about everything that happened during the day and listen to my heart. I lived close to Barceloneta beach. In the past, Barceloneta was just a fishing village with small and typical Spanish houses, but it became one of the most famous tourist areas of Barcelona after the Olympic games in 1992. It was a very cold autumn night. Winter was coming soon, it was already outside the door. No one was on the beach. I arrived and sat down on the cold sand. I remember I had gloves on, a warm hat on my head to protect my ears, and was wearing a comfortable jacket. It was cold and very dark.

Usually, I would leave the beach around eleven o'clock, but for some reason, that night I stayed on the beach a little longer. It was necessary! I did not know the beach lights were going off at midnight. So, I got scared when they went off, and everything got even darker. The good thing was there were lots of bars and restaurants behind me and their lights were on. By the time the lights went off, there was absolutely no one on the beach. I decided to walk a little bit and sit closer to the sea as I looked at the stars shining and heard the loud sound of the waves. Suddenly, I saw someone coming close to me. It was a young woman who walked toward the water. I saw she wasn't wearing sandals, and then, as soon as she put her feet in the cold sea, she quickly jumped out and put her feet back on the sand. After that, she started walking towards me.

"Hola!" I greeted her in Spanish.

"Hola!" She answered, but with a very strong accent. I realized she might struggle to speak with me in Spanish.

"Do you speak English?" I asked her.

"Yes, I do," she replied to me quickly in excellent English.

At that moment I could not see her very well due to the darkness. However, she got closer, sat down on the sand next to me, and finally we started a conversation. I asked her name and what she was doing there. She told me her name and that she was Dutch and came to the beach because she was playing accordion at a party taking place right there behind us. After our kick off introduction, she curiously asked me what I was doing there alone in the cold and dark evening. Immediately, I thought it would be a great opportunity to talk to her about some of my Barcelona experiences, faith journey and passions in life.

"Well, I work for a company in Barcelona," I started my speech. "But, my passion as a volunteer is to engage in activities that have to do with people. I love to see the beauty and diversity of different cultures and be a bridge between people, supporting them as they ponder life's questions. I enjoy meeting new friends and talking about nature and how we always see there is someone somewhere greater than us loving and helping us to walk on this existential ground."

"Are you Christian?" she asked, interrupting the flow of my speech.

"Yes, I am," I answered and felt the breeze blowing stronger and colder in my face as the night advanced.

"Are you Brazilian?" she asked me.

"Yes, I am," I answered her, but immediately I began wondering why she asked me that question.

"I am also Christian!" As soon as she said that, I could see her joy and perplexity for what was going on. I kept listening to her carefully.

"I was at the party, and for some reason, I felt a strong need to come to the beach, walk and pray a little bit," she said.

"I am not surprised," I said. "These last two years, coincidences like this one have been taking place in my life very often. It is what I have been calling divine appointments." I completed my thought by smiling and feeling an enormous joy for what was happening.

"My passion is to go to Brazil," she said to me. "I would love to do mission in Brazil."

I looked at her face and asked her what the probability was to find a Brazilian and Dutch, both Christians, in Barcelona on a beach at two in the morning. After that, we talked about the meaning of being the Church, that is ultimately to understand what Jesus meant for two or three people to gather in His name, how He would be with them "there", and then "there" (wherever it is), would be the Church! When I saw her putting her knees on the sand, I was already praying for her. I prayed for her in Portuguese. I prayed for her dream and plan to do mission in Brazil. After that, I translated what I said from Portuguese into English. She asked me if she could sing a song. I could not believe the sweet atmosphere that had developed.

We could have celebrated the Lord's Supper at that moment, or baptized someone in the ocean. Indeed, such a divine ambiance was around us.

The cold breeze blew like musical notes as she began to sing a song in English, and then, God's presence filled our hearts. Finally, she got up. I stood up next to her. Quickly we exchanged emails, and after that, I left as she started walking back to the place where she was performing. Two years after that, I was in the kitchen in my apartment in Barcelona when a message popped up on my Messenger in Portuguese. Believe it or not, with surprise and joy, I realized it was the young Dutch woman telling me she was doing mission in Brazil through YWAM. I met with her two more times in Europe, in Amsterdam and Barcelona. The most unexpected encounter was when I was walking along the Danube River in Budapest, Hungary and heard someone call my name. I turned around and saw this same Dutch friend because she was performing at an event nearby! Since then she has traveled to Brazil a few times, has learned Portuguese very well, and as far as I know, has been living in Europe with her husband. I had to stay at the beach a little longer that evening. It was necessary…

This is how Johnna described one of our divine appointments in our newsletter last year:

> We had a rolling suitcase, two backpacks, a bright green stroller and Sophia in tow. One would think we were leaving for a month, but no, this is just a typical short trip with a toddler! Excited and filled with anticipation to be going to Hiroshima to visit dear friends, we walked to the station and boarded the elevator. That's when it happened.
>
> A kind, 50-something woman started talking to us in English. We found out that she works in translation and lives not far from our neighborhood. After a short exchange of phone numbers and emails, goodbyes were said and ways parted. A few minutes later, though, we met in another elevator going to the train platform, and then found out we were taking the same train! Johnna sat next to Naoko (she said to call her "Choco") and it was one of those pleasant conversations that may or may not lead to another encounter

ever again. But then, later that evening, Johnna received an email about our meeting. "It was very nice meeting this morning. I usually do not take that train. Today, I was late because the bus was late, so I thought I had bad luck. But, maybe, I was even lucky. If I was on time just as usual, I would never meet a nice family like you! Right?"

As random as these types of meetings and conversations may seem, they have been an important part of our daily routine. We never knew when a conversation might lead to another meeting or a deeper topic or a light bulb moment or even a piece of healing taking place. We tried to live with open hands, being diligent and focused on our tasks, but leaving enough room for happenstance and coincidence, believing that there is a method to this madness and a loving Creator involved in the details that we cannot see.

If You Are A Skeptic, You Won't Believe This (maybe just skip it)

We started developing a friendship with Naoko from this divine appointment. First, Naoko, her husband and their daughter came over for dinner. After that, Johnna and her daughter started exchanging languages, English and Japanese. Our confidence grew to the point that one night Naoko stopped by our place for a couple hours and shared with us how her daughter had been struggling with depression and suicide thoughts for years due to bullying in high school. That evening in our home, Naoko told us her daughter had again done some things that made her think she was going to take her own life. We had an opportunity to listen to her carefully and wisely choose the best way to express our thoughts and advice. What astonished us the most was the fact that a Japanese person who had only known us a short time was sharing something very personal. The high level of suicide among teenagers and young people has been one of the most dramatic and serious issues in Japan.

By the time we decided to go to Hiroshima, we were not sure if airplane or train would be the most economical and practical way to travel. After struggling with our decision, we finally decided to go by train. Naoko usually does not change trains where we met in

Shonandai station. She is usually not late (in general Japanese people are not late), but she had to go to Shonandai station and was late because it was necessary. Divine appointments. Coincidences. Talks in trains and buses. God is actively working in people's hearts and preparing everything for you and me to be agents of His grace and instruments to encourage, counsel, love and transmit His good news to everyone, even those just passing through our lives.

I started getting together with Brazilian soccer players who play for Yokohama Marinos every Tuesday to study the book of John at Starbucks in Yokohama. A certain afternoon I took the train to go to Yokohama and immediately heard someone speaking on the phone in Portuguese. As soon as he finished his conversation, I went up to him and said, jokingly:

"Hey, be careful when you speak Portuguese - you never know who could understand you." I smiled.

"You are right," he replied.

After we introduced ourselves to each other, we kept talking.

"How long have you been here and where do you live?" I asked him.

"I have been here for a few months and I live in Fujisawa."

"Me too!" I said. "Where exactly do you live?"

"Near Mustuainichidaimae station."

"Me too!" I said. "Where are you going now?"

"Yokohama," he said.

"No way! Me too! Well, I am going to get together with a Brazilian soccer player at Starbucks to study the book of John. Have you ever heard about the book of John? Would you like to join us?"

To make a long story short, Fernando joined us at Starbucks. We had a great talk for almost two hours. We exchanged phone numbers and I also asked one of my friends to help him find a new job because by the time we got to Starbucks, he had told me he was looking for a job. A couple weeks later, Johnna, Sophia and I were in a different Starbucks in the Shonandai area, 45 minutes from Yokohama by train, when someone showed up in front of me.

"Hey! What are you doing here?" I asked.

"I saw you through the window and decided to say hi to you," Fernando said.

I had a chance to introduce him to Johnna and Sophia and since then, we have been in touch. I had to, but not really! It was necessary, but not really. In short, sometimes we had to and it was necessary in order to experience divine appointments.

Chapter 5

Living in a Global World

*"Though I am free and belong to no one, I have made myself a slave to everyone,
to win as many as possible. To the Jews I became like a Jew, to win the Jews.
To those under the law I became like one under the law (though I myself am
not under the law), so as to win those under the law. To those not having the
law I became like one not having the law (though I am not free from God's law
but am under Christ's law), so as to win those not having the law. To the weak
I became weak, to win the weak. I have become all things to all people so that
by all possible means I might save some. I do all this for the sake of the gospel,
that I may share in its blessings."*
Paul (1 Corinthians 9:19-23)

Globalization - An Irreversible Phenomenon

My grandparents never imagined the world as global as it is now.
Actually, thirty years ago, I could have never imagined I would be
where I am right now, doing what I am doing. If someone told me
when I was only ten what I would be doing in thirty years, my
parents would have told me to take a few steps back from that
person, thinking he or she was not mentally well. The fact is that our
world has become small. I follow up news on Brazil, North America,

Europe and all parts of the globe daily and instantly via internet at home or in the train by cell phone. I have not watched TV for years, we live in an instant and digital generation.

Normally, I choose to watch documentaries. I choose news in any language I can understand. I look for lectures about many topics online. Everything is accessible and easy to find on the internet. I study languages online as well. I constantly talk to people and have meetings online. Nowadays, you and most[19] of the people on the planet are doing the same things either on smartphones, tablets or computers. It is a digital era. We never thought we would have the entire world in the palm of our hands. Who predicted this unbelievable digital and technological phenomenon? What else are we going to see in the decades to come? Every year I get more surprised when I face the velocity of globalization in all areas, not just the technological segment.

Who knew a few decades ago that we would have video conference calls with people located in different areas of the globe? Who knew we would be able to call from cell phones to our houses, offices and other cell phones as we walked on the streets and paid only a few cents per minute via Skype or any other tool? Our house phones?! Do you know anyone who still has a house phone?!

What was once a product of fiction movies, used only by NASA, Interpol or FBI, has suddenly become possible for any civilian, any human being in practically any part of the world. With that said, let's talk about the immense advantage of living in a world where technology has developed quickly. It is common sense to affirm how technology has become an important global tool, and therefore, an advantage to our work, social activities and learning process in all areas.

Do you remember Windows Messenger tool? Not long ago, we did not have video chats. I am talking about less than twenty years ago. I used to text everyone through Messenger when I lived in Canada. After a short period of time, Windows Messenger incorporated a video feature, and then we were able to use video

---

[19] In 2018, it's estimated that about 2.5 billion people have smartphones. This is about 28% of the population of the world.

cameras to see each other. I remember a certain afternoon at home in Etobicoke, Canada. I had one window chat open to talk to Spain in Spanish, another one to talk to Brazil in Portuguese, one window to talk to Switzerland in English and one last one to have a local conversation with my Canadian friend in English. For the first time, I felt like I had my feet in different nations at the same time, understanding the Great Commission from a global mindset by living in a global and digital world.

In Spain in 2006, I had my first experience, from Barcelona, preaching to a group of people in Brazil over Skype. In the U.S., I experienced the same thing a few more times. I am sure most speakers, preachers, and teachers have had the same experience. Another example: when Johnna was in Florida and I was in Barcelona, our pre-marital counselor was in La Coruña, Spain, so we decided to do our pre-marital course over Skype. Technology has opened a new communication style for people around the world to interact in an inexpensive and comfortable way. Technology has assumed a very important role in our missiological approach by giving us the ability to reach out to different groups of people and cultures, interacting with them infinitely faster, more efficiently and dynamically than a few decades ago.

Today, for our project in Japan, we regularly use a blog, Facebook, videos, a newsletter in English, Portuguese and Spanish, text messages through our cell phones via local and international applications such as LINE (Japanese app) and WhatsApp (International app). Tools are updated quickly and our generation moves from one tool to the next very fast, therefore, it is crucial to keep up with those changes in order to keep reaching out to the maximum number of people from different angles, always keeping our eyes open in order not to be left behind. Technology and the digital era force us to become chameleons who know how, what, why and when to talk to which group of people. Recently, I noticed that far more people click on our videos than our blog posts. More people answer "like" to our Facebook pictures than read our monthly newsletters. In short, we try to do all that is possible to reach out to the maximum number of people with different lifestyles and generations.

What other important aspects are in a global world? Which characteristics do we find in a person with a global mindset? How can we prepare ourselves to face constant change in our societies? Is there any way to prepare ourselves better? Yes, these questions are a good beginning. The immediate response is it is an advantage, and now almost an obligation, to speak a foreign language in order to succeed in a global world. From a business to a personal perspective, if you do not speak at least English, the universal language in a globalized world, you are out of the professional market or lose opportunities to meet new people, develop global friendships and have access to unlimited information. For example, if you live in Europe and want to be competitive, you should probably speak at least three languages and have a good political, economical and cultural overview of the world.

While in Europe for the first five years, I spoke Portuguese, English and Spanish. After that, as Manager of the International Market, I had to learn French and speak as many languages as possible to develop my role. Are you surprised about my role and challenge to learn as many languages as possible? Do not be surprised! I was not the only one. I was just one more person among many with this profile. While in the U.S. for four years, I spoke English, Spanish and Portuguese working for JP Morgan Chase, and then, Citibank. Once again, I was not the only one, I was just one person among many with this profile. In Japan, Johnna and I get to use English, Portuguese, Japanese, Spanish, French and Italian at different levels, but they are very present and constant in our weekly activities. Paul wrote, "I have become all things to all people so that by all possible means I might save some" (1 Corinthians 9:22).

For Pastors, Church Leaders and Missionaries: Why is a Foreign Language Important?

Today, for any role that someone wants including pastor, evangelist, missionary or church leader, it is extremely important to have language skills. Even though one may not be totally fluent, we need to be studying languages in order to have a more extensive and ample reach, and realize how important foreign languages are in a global worldview. I had an opportunity to study Japanese when I was a teenager for a few months in Brazil. Before I came to Japan, I studied Japanese in the United States for almost a year. As soon as we got to Japan, I studied Japanese intensively for the first four months, between 8-10 hours every day. My study hours were a combination of classroom hours, listening skills exercises in the train, and daily readings at home. It was not easy. Now, I exchange languages when I get together with Japanese people. For example, I teach Spanish for 30 minutes, and then, we practice Japanese for the last 30 minutes. I also have a one-to-one class for two hours a week with a volunteer Japanese professor as part of the Fujisawa City Hall language program.

As I said in a few chapters ago, I am baffled by missionaries who do not experience a total immersion in the culture and language, which they are in. It is extremely vital for any individual to immerse himself or herself in the culture. In our case, Johnna and I would have much more difficulty and make far fewer connections if we did not spend a lot of effort trying to improve our Japanese as much as possible even though our project is considered to be "short-term", as in two to three years. But actually, it is because our season in Japan is short that I study Japanese as much as possible. Where else do you think I could have the best opportunity to study Japanese? When else and where else could anyone improve their Japanese language skills? It is absurd when we hear people say, for example, "Yes, Spanish is very important. I have been in Spain for a few months. As soon as I go back to the United States, I will study Spanish as much as possible, and then I will come back to Madrid and be more prepared to work with native speakers." They rarely do it. Life has a fast rhythm and pace. I cannot even tell you how many times I have heard something like that in these last ten years. Opportunities are rare. We should grab each one of them. We should take advantage of the opportunities in a global world. Years go by and I see these people again, and they have made no progress in the foreign language they said they would go back to the U.S. and study.

I often hear comments from different people such as, "You and Johnna have an advantage because you don't have to learn Japanese. You have a different call in Japan working with people who speak different languages." It can sound like maybe we do not use Japanese as much as missionaries who have been living here for decades. That is true, but not completely. First of all, we understand the importance of the learning process in any culture and the powerful significance of speaking to anyone in their heart language.

Second of all, although we will not be able to speak Japanese as well as our colleagues and other missionaries who have been in Japan for decades, we want to and have been able to speak enough Japanese to communicate with native speakers in our daily activities. But, you may ask me: "Fábio, because you don't speak a high level of Japanese, you will never be able to communicate your personal experiences fully or talk about Jesus as clearly and efficiently as you do in other languages." That is true, but not completely.

Japanese is a "Piece of Cake", Don't You Think?

Our experience is that their attention and respect increase as they hear us trying to communicate as much as possible in their heart language. Although we see them trying to communicate with us in English, we also try to keep asking them questions in Japanese, until they see our efforts and how much we are immersed in the culture and the language learning process. This simple interaction makes a profound and enormous difference to any native speaker in any culture.

I have an interesting story about this phenomenon. As soon as I learned the expression "asa meshi mae" in Japanese that means the same as the idiom, "it's a piece of cake", I started using it to joke with people, saying it was "easy" to learn Japanese. When I met a new person, I always introduced myself, talked about my background and job. Then, since I simply repeated my standard presentation over and over again, almost every day for weeks, I always received excellent feedback about my Japanese. However, everyone who studies foreign languages knows that native speakers give you positive feedback not because you are speaking their language very well, but because they want to encourage you to keep studying it, therefore, they may say: "Your Spanish (or French, Japanese, any language) is excellent!" The fact is, after my "excellent presentation", I started saying "Nihongo, asa meshi mae!" (Japanese is a piece of cake!) They immediately laughed after hearing that, and then I said "jyoudan desu" that means, "I'm joking." So, after using these two expressions as part of my presentation to break the ice, my "new friend" and I would laugh and "get closer." However, after a few weeks of doing this presentation and joke over and over again, I realized Japanese native speakers weren't laughing anymore. Why not?! What had happened? Why did they laugh before and suddenly, it became an "offense?" Johnna told me maybe they started thinking I was saying it seriously in a prideful way and they no longer believed it was a joke since my Japanese was starting to improve. Nevertheless, I still use these phrases when I'm certain others will know I mean it as a joke.

Even if you and I may not be fluent or able to have a deep dialogue with a native speaker, our basic knowledge along with small, but daily improvements and sincere efforts will catch any native speaker's attention and respect, allowing us to develop the minimum level of communication. In addition, let's not forget that our daily actions of how we love and treat our daughter or son, how we talk to our spouses, how we respond to life and how we speak to people in their heart language, even at a basic level of communication, will communicate a more powerful and deeper message than even the most fluent speakers in the world, if they do so without love.

With that in mind, not only because we are disciples of Jesus, but because of a global mindset, we are supposed to respect differences between cultures, be more flexible and understanding regarding possible culture mistakes, be agents who are able to work with plurality and diversity, and through it all, be more compassionate by being aware of the most urgent and serious global events such as unjust wars, horrible acts of terrorism, complex immigration and refugee problems among other political, economical and social issues that are known by most of the world. In short, language skills, technology, and traveling come up as additional important characteristics of this global scenery. I am happy to see how traveling has become much easier and cheaper these last two decades. For example, I was twenty-two years old when I flew to Italy and Israel. It was my first time flying in life. It was so expensive, I thought I would never fly again. But now, Sophia just turned three and has already flown more than 40 times! The traveling phenomenon has become an amazing opportunity to get together with family, people we met before, do our work and reach out to a greater number of people.

Global Mindset - An Emerging Profile

I remember when I met Christopher from Switzerland in Canada in 2000. We studied English together in Toronto. I was already beginning to be exposed to the global mindset. When I was a teenager, I never thought I would go to Canada and meet a Swiss person who would speak five languages. When I met him, his background and language skills amazed me. After that, we kept in contact through emails and Messenger. After a few years, I saw him in Switzerland again. We acknowledge how the technological phenomenon and English as our common language have been the catalyst for our friendship. Years later, we met up in Amsterdam and Barcelona. By the time I moved to Europe, we had switched from Messenger to Skype, which became our main technological resource. Christopher came to my engagement party in Barcelona and before Johnna and I moved to Japan, he and his girlfriend, who is French, came to visit us in Florida. Now you can see how the traveling phenomenon brings our lives much closer to each other than we thought they would be. I do not know where and when we will get together next, but I know that language, technology and traveling have all played a constant role in our friendship since 2000. Honestly, back then, I never thought our friendship would take this shape. However, today, I know if I meet a new person, I may see him or her somewhere and somehow in the future. In short, the global world has made our lives much more accessible to one another even when we are miles and miles apart geographically.

I met Peter in La Coruña, Spain. Peter was a short-term missionary in Spain. Actually, Peter and my wife, Johnna, were colleagues working for Covenant World Mission in Europe. After that, Peter became my roommate in Barcelona and we spent two years working on a church-planting project. We baptized our first person, Joy, on Barcelona beach. Joy went back to the United States. Peter went back to the United States, too. They got together again in Chicago. And then, they got married. Well, Johnna and I decided to get married in Chicago and then move to Florida. Peter and Joy came to a local Jazz Club in downtown Chicago to welcome me a few days before Johnna and I got married at Immanuel Covenant Church. Peter was our guitar player in the wedding celebration. Still, our meetings did not end in Chicago.

Peter and Joy moved to Seoul, Korea. Johnna, Sophia and I moved to Japan. A few months ago, we all got together (Johnna, Sophia, me, Peter and Joy) in Hiroshima because coincidentally, they were traveling in Hiroshima when we happened to be there. Recently, we had the chance to go to Seoul and visit them. One more city, one more different culture, and it probably will not be the last time or the last culture or city. What I am describing here is not just a personal experience. Rather, it is a global experience that thousands and thousands of people are participating in right now, and, undoubtedly, this global mindset is increasing all around the world.

In summary, foreign languages build bridges of communication with others, technological tools make it easy to keep in touch and today, more than ever, the feasibility of traveling everywhere has become the foundation for the new global society. All these global ingredients together offer us a powerful instrument to connect to people, develop friendships as we also share our faith in Jesus, live our existential journey and become agents of reconciliation by God's grace. We absolutely can say like the apostle Paul, "I have become all things to all people so that by all possible means I might save some. I do all this for the sake of the gospel, that I may share in its blessings" (1 Corinthians 9:23).

The Apostle Paul Was a Global Citizen (2,000 years ago)

Which characteristics and tools were used in the lives of the apostles that made them more efficient in their ministries? What did the apostles do in those days to spread the message of Jesus? Let's take a quick look at Paul and his ministry. Even 2,000 years ago, he already had a global mindset. Paul could be a citizen of our current globalized world and it would challenge us to do better. He was an extraordinary, intelligent and eloquent man. He was born in Tarsus, part of what is currently Turkey. In Acts, we find out a little more about his background. It says, "I am a Jew, born in Tarsus of Cilicia, but brought up in this city. I studied under Gamaliel and was thoroughly trained in the law of our ancestors" (Acts 22:3a). Therefore, Paul probably spoke Turkish because he was born in

Tarsus, Latin because he was a Roman citizen, Hebrew and Aramaic because he was Jewish, and also Greek that was considered the universal language for those days, similar to the role English plays in the world today.

How could Paul also be a Roman citizen? Luke wrote, "the commander ordered him to be brought into the barracks, and said that he should be examined under scourging, so that he might know why they shouted so against him. And as they bound him with thongs, Paul said to the centurion who stood by, 'Is it lawful for you to scourge a man who is a Roman and hasn't been condemned?' When the centurion heard that, he went and told the commander, saying, 'Take care what you do, for this man is a Roman.' Then the commander came and said to him, 'Tell me, are you a Roman?' He said, 'Yes.' The commander answered, 'With a large sum I obtained this citizenship.' And Paul said, 'But I was born a citizen.' Then immediately those who were about to examine him withdrew from him; and the commander was also afraid after he found out that he was a Roman, and because he had bound him" (Acts 22:24-29, NKJV).

In this passage, we observe that Paul took advantage of his Roman citizenship. I am not surprised. I was born in Brazil so I have a Brazilian passport, but lived in Spain for almost six years and became a Spanish citizen. The fact that I married Johnna, an American citizen, and lived in the United States, allowed me to also became an American. You probably already figured out that I do not need a visa to go almost anywhere, because one of my three passports covers me legally to stay in almost any country for at least three months. Welcome to the global world!

The apostle Paul has an inspiring personality and is my favorite thinker. He spoke several languages and used his knowledge in philosophy, different cultures, his religious Pharisee background, Jewish history and even his Roman citizenship to establish common ground and announce Jesus and his resurrection. If Paul was able to take advantage of a not-yet-globalized world 2,000 years ago, how could I use his life as an example to think of missiology in a total global environment? In reality, when I talk to individuals who come from Sri Lanka, Japan, Brazil, Italy, Egypt, Saudi Arabia, Spain, China or any part of the world, I look for what we might have in common in order to make my approach to them. Obviously, my first step is to find a language we have in common. After that, a common city we have visited, a historical or political event we have studied or heard about, or even our current common culture, political, social, religious or economical context may become the basis for our very first conversation. Finding common ground to start our conversations is essential.

Recently, I went to meet a friend at Denny's near our house in Fujisawa, Japan. Yes, Denny's! You read it correctly. It is part of globalization - Denny's is in Japan! Well, I talked to my Sri Lankan friend in English about the projects he worked on in Korea a few years ago. I asked him questions about his current studies in Japan. He has been working on a similar project in Japan for a year. It is a post-doctoral project and he is a researcher. My point is that you and I should ask people questions about what they do, what they study, what they are interested in. In this case, my Sri Lankan friend and I keep developing our friendship as he and his wife, both Hindu, continue to come to our International Hangout on Thursdays. How often do people ask you questions about what you do? How often are you interested in knowing what your neighbor is feeling about his new job? How many times do you say hi to the couple of foreigners who live next door?

I know we should not be intrusive in certain cultures. I know my first talk with a Brazilian is different than a first talk with a Japanese person. I am aware of the fact that a first talk with a Spanish person is different than with a Swiss person even though they are both Europeans. I know as a Brazilian, due to historical and cultural reasons, it is easier for me to talk to someone from the Middle East than it is for someone like my wife who is from the United States. But, in all cases, it is about being sensitive and showing a true interest in building bridges, caring for people and their lives. There is not one culture that is able to resist our love and sincere care.

How can we identify the common ground? How can we discern how to talk and what to talk about? Is there a manual to follow with three to five steps to know exactly what I should do when I meet someone at Starbucks or in the train station? How should I talk to my neighbor who is a refugee or immigrant? This is your journey. This is my journey. This is your task. This is my task.

I am constantly thinking about ways to talk to people: introduce myself first, ask them questions, tell them I am from Brazil, ask them where they are from, discern their needs, help them, etc. It depends on the current culture and country in which we are immersed. It depends on what we like to do, what we are interested in learning, what kind of people we meet, where we meet them, etc. Because of all of the variables, we should know ourselves and observe how to establish bridges between people and cultures as we meet them for the first time. We should discern people's backgrounds and be sensitive to them, knowing when and how to go deeper in conversation and friendship in spontaneous and natural ways. When is it appropriate to bring up Jesus and my spiritual journey when I meet someone for the first time? When is it appropriate to talk about what I do in detail as soon as I meet someone for the first time? It depends. But, usually I try to ask questions and then naturally, we end up talking about personal things. I almost always have a chance to share about my personal spiritual journey once Jesus has been separated from any type of religious package.

How is the common ground factor seen in Jesus's own ministry? How can we learn from his example? Jesus always took advantage of his context to speak through parables. He established common ground. He highlighted roles that were present in 1st century Palestine such as masters and slaves, fathers and sons, farms and workers, using figurative language that was well known and understood by everyone. Jesus took advantage of these connections to speak to people's hearts. In addition, Jesus used what was around him as he walked to transmit his message regarding God's kingdom, forgiveness, hypocrisy, generosity and compassion among other teachings. He used nature to provide examples and sources for his analogies such as fig trees, birds, lilies of the fields, etc. How can we also use practical examples from our lives to connect with those around us? How can we apply these concepts in our daily journey? How can we find common ground that allows us to speak of our faith and journey with Jesus?

For instance, let's say I meet an Argentinian in Europe. Since we both come from countries that were colonized by Christians with Latin root languages, we would probably speak to each other in Portuguese or Spanish. We could talk about how Portuguese and Spanish colonizers committed atrocities through catechization on behalf of what they called Christianity. Finally, we could discuss the current political and religious fanaticism that are related to ISIS and terrorism in Europe and the Middle East, and continue from there to more global issues. We could eventually end our conversation talking about Jesus, taking him out of these religious-social-political packages and focusing on his life and simplicity, concluding that he has encouraged us to love our neighbors despite their cultural background, and to live life as a peacemaker according to his teachings in the Gospels. It sounds like something complicated, but it is not. It flows naturally, when we do not have "the obligation" to preach. Our lives are the living message. Our love and care will be noticed by anyone, everyone, as we live our faith and journey sincerely.

A couple of weeks ago I met someone in our English gathering in Kamakura. Yesterday, we got together with a different group of people for a barbecue and he told me how he had been looking for philosophical and Buddhist talks and gatherings, but as soon as I talked about Jesus and my meetings with professional Brazilian soccer players studying the book of John, he said: "No thank you!" Until I removed Jesus from the Christian religious package, he was not able to listen to me. As soon as I led him to the historical Jesus and his life, the ambiance changed because he knew he was being provoked to think about Jesus separately from any religion including Christianity as a political and religious event. Finally, he could put Gautama Buddha next to Jesus, next to any other guru or philosopher, and make his own conclusions.

By this time, you probably know the difference between being a christian as fruit of a religious phenomenon and what it means to be a Christian as follower of the Christ. If not, please keep reading…

Unfortunately, throughout centuries, Christianity has transmitted a very negative message to millions of people. Although it is sad to see how Christianity as a religious phenomenon has been a disservice to the true cause of the Gospel, I frequently take advantage of Christianity in history and use its negative and damaging message in my favor in order to point to the historical and real Jesus. There has not been a single occasion where I wasn't able to share Jesus and be listened to as long as I separated the religious movement, Christianity, from the Christ of the Gospels.

It is not difficult when talking to people who are in the U.S., Brazil or Latin America to bring up examples of politicians in those places who assume a Christian viewpoint. It is obvious we are surrounded more than ever by Evangelical fundamentalists in our Congresses and Senate chambers.

I always take their speeches and use them as examples to let my interlocutor know that those speeches, ideologies and anger are absolutely the antithesis of what we observe in Jesus, his teachings, and life. With that, their resistance goes away, and the historical Jesus has an opportunity to be introduced to each one of them, and a face-to-face experience with Jesus in the Gospel narratives becomes a possibility. It seems Luther tried to follow the exact same principle in the Reformation movement by translating the Scriptures and giving the opportunity for Germans to read the Bible by themselves, and over all, interpreting the simplicity of Jesus and his life without any clerical interference.

So, as we conclude this chapter, what prompted me to say "a common ground could be built between *almost* everyone?" Why did I use the word "almost?" Because I am excluding unreachable peoples, cultures, small villages and tribes that have yet to receive any or strong global influence. We cannot compare those unreachable areas to cosmopolitan cities that have received a global overdose from different cultures, tastes, languages, idiosyncrasies, habits and cuisines, having been mixed and overlapped creating an unimaginable heterogeneous and diverse environment. What can we learn from the early church in Acts? Do we have any example of the apostles having discernment to bring out a cultural, historical or other topic to provide a springboard to proclaim Jesus and his resurrection? What I observe in the life of the apostles is the fact that they understood the culture, religious, historical and even geographical backgrounds and contexts in order to talk about Jesus and his resurrection.

Have you realized that the apostles brought up Moses, the prophets, the historical Jewish events and connected them to Jesus only when they were in a Jewish context? On the other hand, if they were in a non-Jewish context talking to Romans, Greeks or Gentiles without Jewish influence, they did not bring up anything about Isaiah, Malachi, Zephaniah or Haggai. Who were these names to those people? Who were Isaiah, Malachi, Zephaniah or Haggai in a Roman or Greek context? No one had any idea. The same principle applies to those unreachable tribes and distant villages on any island in the Pacific Ocean.

Why would a Mongolian need to know that Jephthah was one of the judges of Israel? Why would a Vietnamese person from a small fishing village need to know about the king Rehoboam? And how about a chief in a tribe in the midst of the Amazon jungle; is it essential that he knows about Leviticus and the Jewish rituals? Why do we have to bring up a totally different cultural context about historical Jewish events and unknown characters to indigenous people who have no idea who Abraham or Joshua were?

Why do we have to teach about Saul and his hypochondria, the sacrifices that are described throughout almost all of Leviticus, the Jewish captivity in Babylon, and the conflicts between the Samaritans and Jewish people? It is not necessary. In short, if there is no need to bring up the entire historical Jewish heritage, I do not bring it up. It is not a coincidence that missiological organizations often choose to translate only the New Testament for distant tribes and unimaginable people who live in the intestines of the earth, letting them have access to the historical Jesus and his teachings. When I talk to Japanese people who have a global mindset, our common ground might be discussing Christianity as a religious phenomenon and its implications, but I do not bring up the Old Testament to start a conversation about the historical Jesus if they don't have any background with it. I announce the historical life of Jesus according to the New Testament and how he lived and taught. In short, the Living Word of God, Jesus, and his Good News are what really matter.

Do you remember what happened in Acts in the Areopagus with the apostle Paul (Acts 17)? I like how Paul quoted the Greek philosopher there in Athens. By the way, when Paul was in a non-Jewish context, he focused on non-Jewish existential topics such as slavery, freedom, self-control and many other topics, directing the conversation to end up announcing Jesus, his resurrection, the power of the Gospel to overcome any fear (including fear of death), guilt or evil accusation. He proclaimed the good news as unconditional love from an eternal God who chose to become flesh and dwell among us.

Now how about the Gospels? Can we see this same discernment in Matthew, Mark, Luke and John? Did they do anything to get closer to their audiences? In the Gospels, we observe the same principles. Matthew starts with a meticulous genealogy of Jesus. His audience is Jewish people in a Jewish context. Mark, however, does not mention anything about Jesus' genealogy. Why? Because his audience wasn't Jewish - they were generally Romans and Gentiles. What would those people gain from hearing Jesus' genealogy? It wouldn't mean anything to them.

I'm realizing more and more that our work should be to show the historical Jesus and the simplicity of his message. Geographical, cultural, historical and religious factors are important indicators to tell me what I should or should not bring up in conversation. Those of us who are immersed in a Judeo-Christian society are often not able to see the subtle yet extremely important differences between external and cultural factors. Most people do not know the Jesus who is presented in the Gospel. They have just heard through others' interpretation about "a certain Jesus" even though we live in a globalized world with a strong Christian influence and heritage. They have heard about a certain Jesus who came from a Western religion. A certain Jesus who is connected to Christianity and its discrepancies such as wars, tyrannies, holy inquisitions, crusades, connections between priestly and political power, moral laws and doctrines that say what to do and what not to do.

A young atheist may have grown up with a father who was a pastor. He never read anything in any of the Gospel narratives. Everything that he knows about Jesus was the result of his father's sermons and speeches. Because his father did not coherently live out what he was preaching, this young man had a huge misconception and misunderstanding of Jesus and his true message. A young lady who comes from an emotionally and spiritually abusive background was taught if she did not go to church, she would go to hell. Church became a nightmare to her when she grew up. She heard about Jesus, she was taught a bunch of rules, what to wear, what kind of music she could listen to, and an endless number of moral rules. Has she ever been exposed to the Jesus who welcomed children, acted in love and never imposed any moral rule? She may not even know how Jesus was vehemently against any type of religiosity and hypocrisy. In short, it is no surprise how resistant she has become to our talks when we meet together and talk about faith, Jesus and church.

I can give you multiple examples like these. As soon as we start talking with someone who fits this profile, they can quickly perceive the incoherency and incompatibility of the god of Christianity and the true historical Jesus from the Gospel as we keep comparing both characterizations of Jesus side by side. Today, unless we make this break between the two different characterizations, unless we work on this clear and precise difference, we probably will not have many chances or opportunities to capture people's attention to listen to us share about Jesus and his life in any part of the world. We should acknowledge that we definitely live in a post-Christian society.

Christianity (the religion) Has Built Many More Walls Than Bridges

How should we analyze the most influential Christian countries of the world? How much have they been contributing to produce a post-Christian society? Why have we had difficulty penetrating people's hearts when we introduce ourselves as Christians in a global world? What are the main reasons that have led to an entire generation with antipathy toward Christian beliefs? I could write another book on my own experiences and hundreds of historical facts to explain this phenomenon. But in brief, we could analyze, for example, how our evangelical churches are ironically "full" of people in Latin America, but in reality, the people are "empty", lacking awareness of the full gospel. This phenomenon started in the '90s. We had a strong historical denominational influence and good theologians at that time. However, near the end of the '90s, our pentecostal temples and churches began exploding with thousands and thousands of people. Our gospel concerts and events like March for Jesus in Brazil[20] started bringing millions of people to the streets. However, the Gospel and the message of Jesus became diluted. The most recent Brazilian political scandals have involved evangelicals who are steeped in corruption. Most of the pastors and leaders who have been marching on the streets and leading the "biggest

---

[20] I participated in a few Marches for Jesus in Brazil in the 1990s. Unfortunately, the prosperity Gospel grew quickly and hit most of the charismatic denominations including the March for Jesus leaders. Noting a short article about this movement in Brazil, http://www.christianitytoday.com/ct/2010/august/1.16.html

evangelical event of the world", and are in charge of TV programs, radios and magazines, have been accused of manipulation, extortion and money laundering in their churches.

It has been said that after an average of five years, people who have been attending these churches become atheist or agnostic and no longer want to hear anything related to the Evangelical movement, God, Christianity or Jesus. Why? Because they were never introduced to the simplicity of the Gospel and Jesus. They have been introduced to a "Jesus" who is able to solve their financial problems and give them successful careers. They were basically promised that they would never even have an ingrown toenail. During the last couple decades, no matter where I have traveled or lived, I have met multiple people with this profile. This is due to the fact that over the last couple decades, most Christian Latin American countries have been influenced greatly by prosperity theology, and then, most of the charismatic churches have exacerbated the meaning of the power of Jesus' blood. It has nearly become a magic mantra, sweeping an obscure syncretism into churches that made millions of people look at Jesus as an object or vending machine from which to obtain their greatest desires. As a result of that, an enormous number of people outside the Evangelical movement began looking at this type of Christianity with repugnancy. Unfortunately, still referencing the Latin American context, the historical churches have lost much of their influence in recent decades, especially due to the fact that charismatic and pentecostal churches own the media. Therefore, through the use of TV and radio, magazines and internet, charismatic leaders have been able to attract multitudes to their temples in order to "sell" their promises of hope, prosperity and healing on behalf of Jesus. Personally, this scenery has become one of the most interesting political, religious, anthropological and social phenomena to be studied.

The Megalomaniac, Messianic, Ideological Project to Conquer the World for Christ

The political evangelical ideology in the United States has been producing the same repugnancy for millions of people who no longer want to hear anything related to Jesus or Christianity in America.

Does this match your experience? How do your friends react to you when you say you go to church or that you are a Christian? Is it ok to talk about Jesus with your colleagues without them mentioning something that recently happened in politics involving one of the conservative evangelical politicians and their evangelical ideologies? American mega churches, sharing much in common with enormous malls, have in general, built many more walls than bridges in North America. Most of these anthropocentric theologies have been exported from the United States to Latin America and Africa. Most of the sexual scandals involving "famous evangelists" have come from the United States. In a few decades, the US will be close to the reality of European post-Christian society. My guess is that you already know what has been written throughout hundreds and hundreds of years on the pages of history in Europe. Christianity, as a religious phenomenon in Europe, was dead a long time ago. The historical, political and religious European events seen side by side for centuries led to the creation of a post-Christian society and an automatic repugnancy toward religion as felt by the new and young generation of Europeans. For example, dictators walked side by side with the Catholic church. Franco in Spain, Salazar in Portugal. Horrible things happened under repression, torture, and killing in Spain and Portugal as the Catholic church turned a blind eye to unbelievable atrocities and continued as a political partner with those dictatorships. What to say of Italy? The Vatican is the last bastion of the Roman Empire. It is the last political-religious representation remaining from those years of Roman Emperor tyranny and the force of a political-religious institution that has been involved in countless sexual, political and economic scandals.

I could go on and on. France produced a skeptical society after the influence of the Enlightenment and its intellectual thinkers and philosophers. Jean-Paul Sartre, the French atheist and existentialist philosopher, is one of those main influences. Several Protestant churches have become mosques in England. The United Kingdom faces a period of Christian decadence and complete lack of Christian examples or references. It is impossible to deny how far away from their Reformation roots are countries such as Germany, Switzerland, and the Netherlands. Wherever you go in the world today, you will likely meet people who are hurt and burned out due to some of these influences that have become well known due to globalization. So, how can we present Jesus as He is? How can we help people overcome their repugnancy? How can we demystify the wrong image of Jesus and bring people to the simplicity of his teachings? What should we do when we meet those who attended church for years and then became atheists? How about those who come from a religious and abusive family background? There is just one answer. We should present Jesus through the Gospel and its narratives. That is it. It is as simple as that. Every person who reads about Jesus should be given the chance to decide who He is. Everyone who reads about Jesus through the Gospel narratives should say who Jesus is to him or her.

I notice that even among communities of believers, we have lost the appetite for reading the narratives of Jesus. We have theological discussions, we listen to well-known pastors and preachers, but the reality is that most who claim to be believers in Jesus barely read the Gospels themselves nor spend time reflecting on them. It is supposed to be a constant exercise of reflection, having the words in our mind, memorizing Jesus' teachings, and observing carefully how he responded to life, believing in his miracles, trying to contextualize his examples and parables. Jesus is the hermeneutic key to our existential and spiritual journey. He used a prophetic-love hermeneutic and demonstrated to humankind how to love God, neighbor and life. With that said, our job - mine and yours - is to take every single person we meet on life's road and lead each of them to the main source, the narratives of Jesus in the Gospels. Without realizing it, we will find we are taking them one step closer to Jesus.

Then what? What's next? You may be thinking, "Fábio, you will lose connection with these people. You can't possibly follow up on everyone's spiritual journey." Do you believe in the Holy Spirit? Now it is my sincere question to you. Do you? Who is in charge? Who has control? What is your role? What is God's role? Are you able to convince someone about his or her sins and condition to surrender his or her life to the One who is able to give them hope and joy? Believe me. Let God be God. He will be the One taking care of every single person as soon as they start reading the fascinating, extraordinary and incomparable life of Jesus and observe you and me living out what we truly believe.

Chapter 6

Why Japan?

"To humans belong the plans of the heart, but from the Lord comes the proper answer of the tongue."
Solomon (Proverbs 16:1)

It All Started in our Living Room in Florida

It was my first week in Clearwater, Florida. Finally, home sweet home. Johnna and I had spent hours and hours talking to each other over Skype and had written thousands of emails to one another. We met in Europe when I was in Barcelona and she was in Waterloo, Belgium. By the way, I do not recommend to anyone to have a long distance relationship. "Why?!" you ask? You may be thinking, "But it worked great for you guys!"

Well, you are right, but this does not mean it will work for you or somebody else. We do not have a secret ingredient, no magic formula. Although we live in a digital era, online chats are not the most efficient way to resolve conflicts or get to know your boyfriend/girlfriend well. In our case, we had to be creative to keep our relationship alive, dynamic and fun. I remember we once planned to watch a movie "together." I went downtown Barcelona and Johnna went downtown Brussels. We watched *Invictus*, the story of Nelson Mandela through the eyes of a rugby season one afternoon at almost the same time in different movie theaters. I chose my seat, got some popcorn and a coke, and then, I pretended that Johnna was next to me. We texted during the movie, and later continued the discussion over Skype. Other times we had coffee together. We bought our pastries and grabbed a cup of coffee or tea and sat in front of our computers talking to each other as we ate our breakfast "together." Today, it sounds kind of fun, but it was both fun and hard at the time. Nevertheless, we did not have a different choice in that season to develop our friendship. Then, things got even more complicated. Johnna had to return to the United States to work through some personal issues. During that time, we were on different continents, in different time zones, for over a year. Johnna and I could tell you how difficult that particular season became and how we had to be extremely intentional in our decisions and relationship, overcoming each obstacle one by one, on that tough and stony road in our journey.

Why was the next step Florida? Why the USA? Why not Europe? First, Johnna was already back in the United States. Second, we decided to get married in Chicago near where most of Johnna's family was living, and after that, we decided to live in Florida because Johnna's mom and sisters lived in Tampa Bay. So, back to our Clearwater home sweet home. It was only our first week at home in Clearwater and we had just returned from our honeymoon. As I waited for my green card to start working in the United States, I became a home executive taking care of our apartment, cooking and cleaning while Johnna worked for a consulting company. One day in the kitchen, Johnna came to me and said:

"Fábio, I just saw something interesting on the Covenant website. The post says that Japan needs people speaking Portuguese, Spanish, English and some Japanese…"

"No way," I immediately interrupted her. "I just came from Spain to the United States to marry you. I'm not moving to Japan as a missionary! Are you kidding me?!"

A Random Job Description

At the time Johnna read the post in question, the Covenant

denomination that has been in Japan more than fifty years, had never had anyone working specifically with the Brazilian-Japanese and Latino-Japanese communities. In fact, it was likely they were wondering if anyone could meet this specific need. You might now be asking yourself, "What is the connection between Brazil, Latin America and Japan? How did they become so connected to each other if they are so far from one another and have so many cultural differences?" I was asked this question over and over again in the United States as we spoke at many churches and meetings before coming to Japan. Maybe you have heard that Brazilians constitute the largest number of Portuguese speakers in Asia. The largest numbers in Japan are concentrated in Toyota[21] and Oizumi,[22] where it is estimated that 15% of the population speaks Portuguese as their native language, and Hamamatsu, which contains the largest population of Brazilians in Japan.[23] Brazilians are not particularly concentrated in larger cities such as Tokyo or Osaka. They tend to live where there are large factories.[24] In addition, Tokyo has the largest carnival parade outside of Brazil.[25] Portuguese is the third most spoken foreign language in Japan, after Chinese and Korean,

[21] "Brazilian community in the Homi Danchi, Toyota City" at http://www.mutantfrog.com/2009/03/10/brazilian-community-in-the-homi-danchi-toyota-city/

[22] See "Exploring Oizumi, Japan's little Brazil," http://the-japan-news.com/news/article/0003562605

[23] From the Hamamatsu City Newsletter "Little Brazil: Hamamatsu and the Japan-Brazil Year of Exchange 2008," http://www.city.hamamatsu.shizuoka.jp/foreign/english/newsletter/no5.html

[24] See "A new documentary shows the surprising, circular journey of Japanese Brazilians" https://www.pri.org/stories/2016-04-22/new-documentary-shows-surprising-circular-journey-japanese-brazilians

[25] See http://www.unmissablejapan.com/events/asakusa-samba-carnival

and is among the most studied languages in the country.[26] Japan has four Brazilian newspapers in Portuguese along with Portuguese radio and television stations.[27] Brazilian fashion and bossa nova music are also popular among Japanese.[28] Very often, one can hear bossa nova in cafes and restaurants throughout Japan. Yesterday, Sophia and I were at Starbucks. As she took her nap, I worked. When she woke up, I said to her, "Sophia, listen to this music! You and daddy might be the only people in here who understand what they are singing!" I said that because the music was a beautiful bossa nova song. Sophia smiled at me as she kept drinking her chocolate milk.

Why are Japanese people in Brazil and why are Brazilians in Japan?

What are the historical facts behind these phenomena? Why, when, and how did this immigrant exchange happen? A few historical facts as a quick summary:

> 1850 – At the end of the 19th Century and the beginning of the 20th, coffee was Brazil's main export. In order to harvest the large amounts of coffee beans, Brazil used slave labor from

---

[26] Although this connection between Brazil and Japan is easy to understand from the Brazilian perspective, (since Brazilians grow up around second-generation Japanese people), I know for most of my foreign friends, it seems like a utopia. I chose a short, but excellent blog that shares statistics, historical context and problems related to Brazilian-Japanese people in Japan. See "Life as Dekkasseguis: The Brazilian Community in Japan" http://www.hurights.or.jp/archives/focus/section2/2009/12/life-as-dekkasseguis-the-brazilian-community-in-japan.html

[27] For more, see "Hamamatsu Journal; Sons and Daughters of Japan, Back From Brazil" http://www.nytimes.com/2001/11/27/world/hamamatsu-journal-sons-and-daughters-of-japan-back-from-brazil.html

[28] For more, go to: http://www.correiodoestado.com.br/noticias/japao-imigrantes-brasileiros-popularizam-lingua-portuguesa/43355/

Africa. In 1850, when slavery was abolished, Brazil began to bring in Europeans, especially Italians, to work in the fields. However, due to poor working conditions and low salaries, the Italian government was forced to interfere with the relationship between Brazil and Italy, making the migration of Italians to Brazil more difficult. In 1908, Japanese workers starting coming to Brazilian coffee plantations[29] to fill the hole in the workforce left by the Italians.[30] Today, it is estimated there are over 1.8 million Japanese descendants in Brazil.[31]

1980 – Brazil faced an ongoing economic crisis while Japan experienced growth and strength. Thousands of Brazilians with Japanese ancestry migrated to Japan.[32]

1990 – The Japanese government realized many immigrants had arrived illegally. They decided to open the doors to those with Japanese decent going back three generations. This decision allowed many immigrants to receive legal documents. Also, since Brazil has the largest number of Japanese people outside of Japan,[33] Japan attracted another wave of Brazilians with Japanese descent in the 1990s. It is worth noting that the majority of Brazilian immigrants working in Japan are

---

[29] "Mixing sushi and samba - meet the Japanese Brazilians," by Milena Veselinovic, for CNN on http://edition.cnn.com/2013/06/11/world/brazil-japanese-community/

[30] *Mass Migration to Modern Latin America* by Samuel L. Baily, Eduardo José Míguez, p. 122.

[31] *Mixing sushi and samba - meet the Japanese Brazilians* by Milena Veselinovic, for CNN on http://edition.cnn.com/2013/06/11/world/brazil-japanese-community/

[32] *Asia and Latin America: Political, Economic and Multilateral Relations*, edited by Jörn Dosch, Olaf Jacob, page 74.

[33] Taken from "The Brazilians winning in Japan" by Ewerthon Tobace. BBC Brasil, Tokyo on http://www.bbc.com/news/business-33114120

working in industries that are not so attractive to Japanese natives. Most of them settle outside of major cities where there are factories and farms. Aichi and Gunma prefectures tend to have the most Brazilians because of their factories.[34]

2009 – The financial crisis hit the world. The global financial crisis also hit Japan causing many people to lose their jobs. This critical economic situation caused many immigrants, especially Brazilians, to return to their home country. The Japanese government offered incentives to all individuals wishing to return to their countries of origin.[35] In the case of Brazilians, the strengthening of the Brazilian economy made the decision to return to Brazil seem like a great opportunity.

As a result of this historical overview, Brazil is home to the largest Japanese population outside of Japan and the community has been growing since the 1950s. The largest concentrations of Japanese people in Brazil are found in the states of São Paulo and Paraná. Liberdade is São Paulo's equivalent of Japan Town in the USA.[36] And why Latinos? Why are there so many Peruvians[37]

---

[34] "Life as Dekkasseguis: The Brazilian Community in Japan" by Erika Calazans http://www.hurights.or.jp/archives/focus/section2/2009/12/life-as-dekkasseguis-the-brazilian-community-in-japan.html And also cited in Latin American Diaspora in the world - Academy for Cultural Diplomacy in Latin America (CDLA) http://www.culturaldiplomacy.org/academy/index.php?en_cdla_diaspora

[35] See "Japan to Immigrants: Thanks, But You Can Go Home Now" http://content.time.com/time/world/article/0,8599,1892469,00.html

[36] See article "Mixing sushi and samba - meet the Japanese Brazilians" by Milena Veselinovic, for CNN on http://edition.cnn.com/2013/06/11/world/brazil-japanese-community/ Cited in Japan Abroad—Japantowns Around the World by Danielle Tate-Stratton on http://www.tokyoweekender.com/2007/11/japan-abroad-japantowns-around-the-world/

[37] The Japanese in Peru: History of Immigration, Settlement, and Racialization

and Argentinians[38] in Japan? Why, in the past, was Shonandai, a neighborhood in Fujisawa, Kanagawa Prefecture, considered to be the most Argentinian neighborhood in Japan? Well, basically due to the same phenomena. First, Japanese people went to Peru and Argentina to work for political, social and economic reasons. Peru is another country with one of the largest number of Japanese inhabitants in the world.[39] And then, the wave of second and third generation Japanese-Latin Americans came to Japan to find a better life and future since Latin America had been struggling economically and socially for decades. Latinos are the second largest group of immigrants in Japan, only behind Asians. The Brazilians and Peruvians represent the largest Latin communities.[40] The Greater Tokyo Area, Chukyo Metropolitan Area (near Nagoya City) and Nagoya City, Hamamatsu, Toyota and Oizumi are the most concentrated areas of Latin Americans in Japan. One of our church partners in Japan has a pastoral couple that represents what I'm talking about. Gabriel, the husband, is Brazilian-Japanese and Neusa, the wife, is Peruvian-Japanese. As soon as we met them, we knew we could use their church as a good example to confirm the historical facts and reality in Japan.

Well, back to Clearwater once again. Why did Johnna tell me about that specific need? Why did she want to go to Japan? Johnna had already spent two years in Japan right after university and loved the culture. She even met the first Brazilian in her life in Japan. Before that, she didn't even know Brazil existed. I am kidding…

Ayumi Takenaka, Latin American Perspectives, Vol. 31, No. 3, East Asian Migration to Latin America (May, 2004), pp. 77-98.

[38] See "Historical Timeline of Japanese Argentine"
http://www.janm.org/projects/inrp/english/time_argentina.html

[39] *Mass Migration to Modern Latin America* by Samuel L. Baily, Eduardo José Míguez, p 134.

[40] *Latin American Diaspora in the world - Academy for Cultural Diplomacy in Latin America* (CDLA)
http://www.culturaldiplomacy.org/academy/index.php?en_cdla_diaspora.

mostly.

At this point, you probably know why she asked me about Japan. The fact is that since I grew up in São Paulo, Brazil (the city with the highest concentration of Japanese people outside of Japan), my best friends were Japanese when I was a kid. I even ended up studying some Japanese as a teenager, took karate and judo and started admiring Japanese culture. In theory, anyone who looks at the need and our experiences would say that it would be a perfect fit: Portuguese, Spanish, English and Japanese influence.

"Fábio, you probably said yes immediately." No, I did not. I immediately told her that I could not jump into a new culture. I was already tired of moving from one place to another, changing languages and having almost no stability. So, how did we end up going to Japan? What changed? After about a year, I came back to Johnna and said:

"Johnna, I have been a tent maker since I was 19. If there is a chance to jump into a new life style as partners with Covenant World Mission, I think now would be a good time. Our daughter is at a good age for this too. If Sophia were a teenager, I would probably not do it. I don't see any problem with embracing this project for two years while we discern where we want to raise Sophia."

"I agree with you," Johnna said, feeling great joy on the inside.

When the Unimaginable Happens

Our Japanese journey was just starting. Johnna got very excited and we started making plans. However it was my first time to work for a non-profit and depend on people's generosity for our stipend and living expenses. Honestly, I did not know how to start the fundraising process. At the time we decided to commit to this project, I was working for JP Morgan Chase in Tampa. I used my vacations to travel and spoke in several places, had meetings and coffee with pastors, presented our project in English, Spanish and Portuguese in churches, sent countless emails and Johnna helped me as she was able to in some of those presentations while also taking care of Sophia. In the middle of all this, I changed my job. I found a better position at Citibank. But, I knew it was just for a short season. I started using my vacation time from Citibank to keep our fundraising going. One weekend, I flew to Chicago. It was the Covenant gathering called Midwinter. A few Spanish-speaking pastors invited me to speak about Project Japan, including the head of CHET (Centro Hispano de Estudios Teologicos)[41] in Los Angeles. My answers were always: "Yes, of course. It would be my pleasure!" Nevertheless, I did not know how to combine our new project to move to Japan and my full time job at the bank. Though I said yes to go to California, I didn't have any more vacation days left at work. The following day, a Monday afternoon, as I left Citibank to go home, I got a phone call.

Fábio?

Yes, it is me.

This is Márcio from the Brazilian church.

Hi, Márcio.

Well, I am calling to invite you to be our associate pastor. You have been preaching to our community for over a year and have never asked anything from our church. So, we have decided to invite you to join our team. (I should add here that when I found a new job at Citibank, I had already been preaching every Tuesday at his church, a Brazilian community in Tampa, for more than a year). I could not believe what I heard - "to join our team?!" They had one pastor and their church did not have more than 35 people attending each week. Most of them were professional cleaners or people who worked in construction and other types of hard labor. I continued with surprise:

Are you kidding me? What is going to be my role in the church?

Nothing. Zero!

What?! What do you mean nothing?

We just want to free you up. Our idea is to give you $1,000.00 per month to help you cover your monthly expenses. You do not even need to show up at church. You are free from your job to finish your fundraising and go to Japan.

I could not believe it! I had tears streaming down my face for 40 minutes in the car on the drive back home. As soon as I got home, I

---

[41] "Centro Hispano de Estudios Teológicos"
http://www.chet.org/english/about/our-history/

explained everything to Johnna. It was clear that Johnna was going to become our main financial resource to pay our monthly expenses while I finished raising the funds to go to Japan. After a year and a half, we had all the funding for Project Japan and I went back to Márcio and over lunch, I thanked him for being such an important piece of our mission:

Márcio, we have everything we need to move to Japan. Thank you so much! I know it is not my business, but, how could the church cover the rent, my salary, the pastor's salary and probably other expenses with the budget?

"I don't know," he said with a smile in his face. "We had some savings because we sold some sound equipment a few years ago. We knew we could cover your salary for a year. Also, we guessed you would be able to raise your support in about a year. So, you guys made it!" he said and I couldn't hold back the tears in my eyes as I looked at him gratefully.

Thank you my brother. I have never heard of anything similar to what I experienced with your community.

From that point forward, I started experiencing what I call "the beginning of the end, and the end of the beginning." Finally, we were able to finish our fundraising, but it was just the beginning of the end. Finally, my tent-making season was over, but it was just the end of the beginning, a new chapter in my life. Finally, we were going to sell our stuff, but it was just the beginning of the end. Finally, we were going to need to say goodbye to our families, friends and churches, but it was just the end of the beginning.

Our journey was about to begin…

Chapter 7

Project Japan

"Now to him who is able to do immeasurably more than all we ask or imagine,
according to his power that is at work within us."
Paul (Ephesians 3:20)

Ichi, Ni, San - Hajimemashou... (One, two, three - let's start)

By the time we arrived in Japan, I had only a glimpse of how our life might be. Johnna knew some basic Japanese (just enough) to communicate a little with everyone since she had lived two years in Gunma. Though I studied Japanese for six months in the United States, I knew the language learning process would be the most difficult thing for me. And I was right. On the other hand, I knew my culture shock would be minimized because our project had to do with Brazilian and Latino-Japanese communities in Portuguese and Spanish, international people and Japanese with international tendencies in English and French as well.

My second concern was how to manage our activities and take care of Sophia at the same time. Sophia's first two years were spent with her grandmother (Johnna's mother) as she acted as nanny while

Johnna and I went to work. I knew it would be a huge change for us without the daily help of Johnna's mother. I was right. In fact, my two main concerns went quickly from just theory to reality as they are the two most difficult challenges we faced in Japan from the first day we landed. Johnna and I studied Japanese at a very good school in Yokohama during our first few months. Actually, Johnna took a quick course for five weeks. She continues language study today with her former teacher from that school, a language exchange where Johnna teaches English and learns Japanese, practicing kanji (Chinese characters that are one of the alphabets used in Japanese) and reading by herself. In my case, I studied Japanese at the same school, but intensively for 6-8 hours a day for the first four months. Well, it was necessary to have this first deep and intense immersion. After that, I studied Japanese by myself and started two language exchanges with Spanish and Japanese. I am also in a program sponsored by Fujisawa City Hall where I have a one-on-one lesson to develop communication skills with a volunteer Japanese teacher two hours a week.

Have we been making progress in the language learning process? Indeed it is a hard language. It was deemed the most difficult foreign language for English speakers to learn in 2015. We have been making progress gradually. We also care about understanding the culture so we keep moving forward in trying to learn more about Japanese mentality. You may ask me, "Why was it so hard to manage family and ministry in your first few months of living in Japan?" The fact is that in our first few months, we were visiting different churches almost every weekend to either speak, play a concert or introduce ourselves to a new group of people, and the lack of a babysitter was evident. Sophia was not used to anyone. No one looked familiar to her, therefore, she wanted to stay next to us all the time. Johnna and I had to translate for each other and played concerts together in churches, community centers and other gatherings, and Sophia wanted to be next to us. Today, as I write this chapter, I'm reminded of a time when Johnna had to hold Sophia with her left arm as she kept playing piano with her right hand only. I could not believe it. It seemed everyone enjoyed seeing how we tried to juggle parenting and our work, admiring the way we worked as a family. On a different occasion, Sophia decided to sit down under Johnna's keyboard and watch a cartoon on my iPhone as we played our concert. It is funny to remember these moments now, but at the time it was challenging to find a path that worked well with a toddler.

Johnna and I have had many talks about this, adjusting many things, compromising other things in order to find balance between our activities, family and Sophia's first months in Japan. We did not want to be known as "successful missionaries" while failing in the most important segment of our lives, parenting. So, after some discussion, we decided to make two local churches our bases: the Brazilian-Japanese church in Portuguese and Japanese (Yamato, Kanagawa), and the Chigasaki Covenant Church (Chigasaki, Kanagawa) only in Japanese. We communicated to both of the leaders that we would attend their services when we did not have to preach or play a concert in another location. Finally, after a few months, Sophia got to know a few teenage girls from our local churches and we were able to start calling these young women to help babysit when we had to go and speak somewhere. For example, when we go to the Latino-Japanese church, the service starts at 3pm and ends at 6pm. We prepare three messages (children, adults and then, after their regular service, we do a seminar for couples and families). It is crucial to have someone playing with Sophia as we do our work there. If it is difficult even for us as adults to stay in one place for several hours, can you imagine how hard it is for a two and a half year old child?

As I sit in my chair and write this paragraph, I can see how we have learned how to overcome our giants, but at the same time, I never expected to experience what I've been experiencing so far in such a short period of time. It seems as if everything flows easy and naturally. It seems as if, on a weekly basis, we meet new people and keep going deeper in our conversations with those we have met before. We currently work with five different groups of people: Brazilian-Japanese, Latino-Japanese, international people, native Japanese, and Japanese with international tendencies (those who have lived abroad and love traveling and/or speaking foreign languages). We have churches we can recommend for each group of people and we take turns ministering in different places in Portuguese, Spanish or English. Very often, we are translated from one of these languages into Japanese. Our main ministry is Evangelism (outreach activities) and Christian formation (preaching, leading family workshops, playing concerts).

Christian Statistics in Japan

How many churches are in Japan? What is the population? Do you have religious freedom to preach? How many people on average attend a Japanese church? You may have some of these questions in your mind. Japan's population is around 127,075,045 people. The last study I read said they have one missionary for every 64,244 people, 7,907 churches and 70% of their pastors are fifty-something years old or older. The last statistics point to 0.5% Evangelical Christians and 35 attendees per church. In spite of these numbers, Japan has religious freedom and missionaries are welcomed. However, Japan is considered one of the largest unreached people groups in the world with twenty-two unchurched cities and 546 unchurched towns.[42]

Tokyo is the capital of Japan, the center of the Greater Tokyo Area, and the largest metropolitan area in the world.[43] It is the seat of the Japanese government and the Imperial Palace, and home to the Japanese Imperial Family. Tokyo is often thought of as a city, but is commonly referred to as a "metropolitan prefecture." The population of this special ward is over nine million people, with the total population of the prefecture exceeding thirteen million. The prefecture is part of the world's most populous metropolitan area with upwards of 35 million people[44] and the world's largest urban

---

[42] Operation Japan Prayer Guide CD, Fourth Edition, 2013. Read the article "Sushi, geisha, ninjas and samurai... hot springs, green tea and cherry blossoms: welcome to the fascinating Land of the Rising Sun!" https://www.om.org/en/country-profile/japan

[43] "World Urbanization Prospects: The 2014 Revision Population Database." United Nations. Retrieved August 10, 2014.

[44] Tokyo Population 2017 at http://worldpopulationreview.com/world-cities/tokyo-population/

agglomeration economy with a GDP of US $1.520 billion,[45] ahead of the New York metropolitan area in 2008. The city hosts fifty-one of the Fortune Global 500 companies, the highest number of any city. Tokyo has been described as one of the three "command centers" for the world economy, along with New York and London.[46]

We are located in Fujisawa. It has turned out to be a very strategic place. We are about forty-five minutes from Yokohama and an hour and fifteen minutes from Tokyo. They are both international cities. We are located in a high and dense Latino-Brazilian-Japanese area. We often speak Portuguese and Spanish in the streets, at metro stations and groceries. We have made Starbucks coffee shops our places to work, holding meetings, language exchanges and weekly language conversation groups. Our lives feel abundant and full, vibrant and dynamic. Johnna and I are "people people" so we love to hang out with people from different backgrounds, cultures and even different points of view. We are very grateful for this extraordinary opportunity to experience God's purpose and timing in one of the most fascinating places in the world.

---

[45] Top 10 Wealthiest Cities of the World by GDP at
https://wearetop10.com/wealthiest-cities-of-the-world-by-gdp/

[46] "World Urbanization Prospects: The 2014 Revision Population Database." United Nations. Retrieved August 10, 2014 and Fortune. "Global Fortune 500 by countries: Japan." CNN. Retrieved July 22, 2011.

Chapter 8

Relational Symbiosis

"Coincidence is God's way of remaining anonymous."
Albert Einstein

When the Supernatural Meddles with the Natural

Coincidence?! Not at all. You may call it coincidence, but you may also recognize that some of our experiences in life are absolutely unexpected and inexplicable from a human point of view. In this chapter, I'll share with you a few stories that compose our monthly newsletters. I would like to give Johnna all the credit for this chapter by recognizing her time, energy and efforts to develop the content of our Project Japan monthly newsletter.

An Unexpected Appointment

It was a typical Thursday morning with Fábio at Chigasaki station, sitting in one of his offices (Starbucks) waiting for Yamato. They meet regularly to exchange Spanish and

*Japanese. A Japanese woman approached him, bent down a
bit to get right in front of him and said, "Mi nombre es Jura."
She continued in Spanish telling him that she heard him
speaking Spanish the week before. She spent time in Paraguay
and wanted to brush up on her Spanish. Was there any chance
she could join his language exchange? Once Yamato arrived,
Fábio asked his permission for Jura to join, and Fábio's
Spanish class suddenly doubled. Every week, we are surprised
to meet someone new and develop relationships that
sometimes go deeper than we could imagine. We are grateful
for countless opportunities to plant seeds and pray for each
one who has been brought our way.*

A few weeks ago, Yamato could not come to our conversation
group, so I was able to talk one-on-one with Jura. Her Spanish is
pretty good. Suddenly I realized our conversation had become a sort
of therapy session as Jura told me about her frustrations and fears in
her job.

A Coincidence and the Beginning of our International Hangout

It was a very hot morning. Summer in Japan is hot. I met a Brazilian
missionary named Fernando in Yokohama. By the time we were
finished chatting, we discovered we had some common friends.
Fernando uses his talents with hip hop dance to be a missionary to
young people who also enjoy hip hop. He explained what he has
been doing in Japan, and we decided to keep in touch. Well, what I
didn't know was, the very afternoon I met him, I went to Starbucks
in Shonandai, near my home to work, answer a few emails and
prepare our weekly agenda. Usually when I see a foreigner, I try to
introduce myself. Japan is such a homogenous culture, there is often
an instant connection when I meet a foreigner.

"Hi, my name is Fábio from Brazil," I introduced myself.

"Hi, my name is Simon. I am from Switzerland," he answered
me kindly.

"Nice to meet you!"

"Nice to meet you, too."

After five minutes of talking to Simon, I found out he was a missionary serving OMF (Overseas Missionary Fellowship), the same organization with whom Fernando, the hip-hop missionary, is serving. I could not believe it. I was able to mention Fernando to Simon and of course he knew him, so we delighted in having a common friend. Simon and I started hanging out and developing a friendship. One morning, an idea came to my mind and I shared it with Johnna.

"Johnna, I would like to do something similar to what I did in Barcelona. We could get people together, share our experiences, play a few songs, and have a meal together. They don't necessarily need to have any church or Christian background." She listened to me carefully. "Well, where can we do it?" she asked me. "I think Simon and Sayaka, his wife, could help us organize this new meeting."

I decided to ask Simon to help me launch what we would call an International Hangout. Me, Johnna, Simon and Sayaka, who is Japanese, decided to use the website meetup.com to publicize this new meeting. Here is part of our online announcement:

What do a Swiss man, a Japanese woman, a Brazilian man and a US Citizen have in common? We get together near Mustuainichidaimae Station (Fujisawa) for a relaxed time of hanging out, playing music, eating food, and discussing topics (philosophy, world news, psychology, social issues, etc) and connecting them to the most fascinating, controversial, mysterious person in history, Jesus Christ. Come join us! Countries represented by our long-term travels: Wales, Japan, Switzerland, Canada, US, Brazil, Spain, Belgium. Languages spoken: English, Japanese, Portuguese, French, Italian, Spanish, Swiss German. Children welcome!

Connecting to Each Other

Rashmi, our Sri Lankan friend, was looking for Japanese classes. Johnna took her to our former language school and signed her up to start in April. She just needs to learn two Japanese alphabets and some basic phrases beforehand. Later that same day, at the gym, we ran into a woman named Tomoko who is becoming a Japanese teacher, but is not yet certified. She asked us if we knew anyone who wanted to learn Japanese with a volunteer (i.e. free!). We connected her to Rashmi, and voila!, they started meeting three times a week. We love to connect people to others and help them find what they need. Rashmi and her husband, Supun, come to our International Hangout. Actually, when they visited the first time, I sat between them and our most faithful member, Tomo.

"It is our first time here," said Supun and Rashmi.

"This is a nice place. I have been here since almost the beginning," answered Tomo.

"I am Hindu and from Sri Lanka," the couple said.

"No problem. I am Buddhist," replied Tomo-san.

A welcoming atmosphere makes it easy for everyone to join in as we have a meal together followed by a song or two, a share from one of the leaders and some time for discussion and reflection. Our kids play in the open area right next to us as we talk to each other in the kitchen, exchanging cultural experiences. Throughout the hangout, we try to highlight the most important matters in life using principles of the Gospel and Jesus' teachings. Last week, we celebrated my birthday and Tomoko, who is already coming to our International Cafe in Kamakura, came to our International Hangout. She brought her daughter and her daughter's friend. Supun and Rashmi were there as well. Here is what Tomoko wrote in her facebook about our last International Hangout "Thank you for welcoming us. Both girls really enjoyed the group! Wonderful hosts and amazing coordinators!"

Supun also put a picture up on his Facebook and wrote: "Nice to have a large number of first timers in our meet-up." We loved seeing him use the word "our", signifying his participation and even ownership of this small gathering. It shows he totally feels part of our group. Another example is with Supun. He is in Japan doing research as part of his job. One of his facebook friends commented on a picture of the International Hangout: "Hi Bro, I don't understand, did you change the lab or what?" His answer was: "Nope! This is just a meeting of multinational people! I am still in the same lab!" We see how a simple gesture, a heart of service and hospitality, an attempt to bring people together and connect to each other can construct bridges between cultures and people by making our differences seem much smaller. Last Thursday, we welcomed six first-timers to our International Hangout. We had people from Sri Lanka, Malaysia, USA, Brazil, Switzerland and Japan. Some of the Japanese people have lived in Wales, Australia, Canada and the USA. Our topic was adoption in Japan and how the country has been opening up more to adoption over the years.

A Snowball Experience

Keiko, the friend we encouraged and helped find a new job, has been coming regularly to our twice-monthly international gatherings at our friends' house. Recently, during one of the talks, the book *The Five Love Languages* by Gary Chapman was mentioned and we heard later from Keiko that she went out and bought it immediately. We have observed how our worlds overlap each other. Our different activities and meetings have become ways to serve people, present them to each other and share our personal faith and spiritual journey with many of them. If you want to understand how Keiko ended up in our International Hangout, I should introduce you to Miura. Miura is a young Japanese lady who lived many years in Australia and now works with a non-profit organization in Fujisawa. She came once to Johnna's English group at Starbucks and has been serving our community and neighborhood as a bridge between different cultures and helping Japanese moms and kids improve their English through classes and events.

Johnna and Miura became close friends due to their similar lifestyle and core values. Well, Miura asked Johnna to participate in a Syrian cooking class that also raised money and collected supplies for Syrian refugees. At that event, Johnna met Keiko. They talked to each other and exchanged numbers, but didn't keep in touch. Until the unexpected happened - a few weeks later, Keiko was at Starbucks and coincidently Johnna, Simon and I were there. Johnna and Keiko recognized each other and started talking about Keiko's job and how she wanted to quit and look for a new one. Johnna gave her some ideas for how to immerse herself in the job search through temp agencies and applications for jobs she might not normally apply to.

Well, we took advantage of the fact that Simon was at Starbucks and we all invited Keiko to join our International Hangout. Since then, she and her daughters come and actively participate in the gatherings. This is what we call a snowball experience - we see our activities, daily routine and life converging and culminating to the same common point. It seems that somehow, almost always, the simplicity of the Gospel is exposed to everyone we meet through different, creative, spontaneous and simple ways.

A Kaleidoscope of Different Colors

Yuna, who comes to Saturday morning English, is now also joining us at the Thursday night International Hangout. Kaito, whom we met on Thursdays, met a guy named Jun, and then both of them came to lunch with us after French conversation on Saturday. We continue to be amazed at how it seems like we are experiencing a type of relational symbiosis in our meetings and activities. It is like looking through a kaleidoscope and turning it to see the colors overlap, creating new and different images, but always related to, and using the same pieces, as the last ones. Another analogy might be a machine with chains and sets of gears that fit each other, passing each other and sometimes touching one another as the wheels turn. As we had hoped when we set up our meetup.com groups, our new friends are migrating from one activity to another, meeting each other and helping to create a deeper community where we get to see one another more often, in different contexts. There is an "easy flow" to it and needs for language learning, international connection and community are being met. It certainly seems like we are in the right place at the right time, using very little energy to set things in motion, and then sitting back to watch these divine appointments take place!

When I see how natural Jesus lived life and how the supernatural power of God fell upon His daily decisions, it makes me see life and ministry as a single sphere, natural and supernatural, ordinary and extraordinary, where both of these realms happen at the same time. Johnna and I just try to have a lifestyle where we are naturally sensitive to observe how God's supernatural power is falling upon our daily conversations and constant encounters.

An Unpredictable Encounter

I discovered an Italian restaurant managed by an Italian guy named Francesco. Almost every week, before I get together with Yuma for our Spanish-Japanese language exchange, I stop by Francesco's restaurant, grab a beer and practice Italian as we chat about our week. So, on New Year's Eve, we thought as a family, it would be fun to have dinner in his restaurant in Fujisawa. Johnna and Sophia had never been there. What we had forgotten, however, was that many restaurants are closed on New Year's Eve in Japan. It is part of the culture, we cannot change it! We walked toward the Italian restaurant not knowing if it would be open. As we got closer, I said, "Hey Johnna, I am not sure if Francesco has opened the restaurant today, let me run ahead and check it out." "No problem," Johnna said as she continued to push Sophia's stroller. Unfortunately, his restaurant was closed and sadly I started walking back to Johnna not knowing what to do or where to go. As I was walking back to Johnna, I saw Francesco!

"Francesco, are you not working today?" I asked him.

"Of course not, no one is working today! By the way, Felice Anno! Happy New Year!" he replied to me.

"No way! Tonight I decided to have dinner with my family at your restaurant. Do you know any restaurants that are open tonight?" I asked him.

"I am not sure, but we are also looking for somewhere to go. Let's have dinner together!" As Francesco was finishing his invitation, his Japanese wife and their three-month-old baby showed up.

Thankfully, we were able to celebrate New Year's Eve all together, both families in a Japanese restaurant near Fujisawa station. We introduced our families to each other, had great conversations, and once again, we could see how coincidences had become part of our routine to meet friends and develop connections with a diverse group of people. Six degrees of separation might seem like an obsolete theory. It implies that everyone is only six or fewer "degrees" away from any other person in the world. We may also call it a "friend of a friend" chain. But this phenomenon tries to explain that we could make connections to any person on the planet in a maximum of six steps.

My favorite season of the year is Christmas. By November, I'm already playing carols at home. I love Christmas! It was Christmas day at Starbucks once again, my favorite place to be at Christmas because they play carols in English all day long. Johnna and I were having a nostalgic chat about past Christmases at various places we had lived as we had our drinks and Sophia took her nap. From our table, I saw a foreigner and decided to introduce myself, as you probably already guessed.

"Hi, my name is Fábio. Merry Christmas!"

"Hi, my name is Ajit. Merry Christmas!" he replied.

"I am from Brazil," I continued our conversation.

"Really? I lived in London and my landowner was Brazilian. His name was Marcos."

"We know a Marcos who is Brazilian who lived in London… but it can't be the same one…" I replied with surprise. We showed him a picture of our friend on Facebook and Ajit was shocked, "That's him!"

After this interaction, Ajit and I kept in touch. We told Marcos, a believer and missionary, about our meeting Ajit at Starbucks. Ajit even said he was "almost" a Christian after his experience with Marcos and their group in London. I "cannot" even explain this enormous coincidence…

Our First Christmas in Japan

We probably played about eleven different concerts in different locations our first Christmas in Japan: churches, houses, community centers. Do you remember Miura who works for a Japanese non-profit? During the Christmas season, she asked us to play music at one of her moms and kids events in a local community center. We enjoyed playing and could share about Jesus' birth and life through songs in a non-church activity. On Christmas day, after meeting Ajit, Johnna and I decided to go to the train station and play guitar and sing Christmas carols outside the station. We were surprised to see that many people slowed down as they walked by us playing and singing carols while Sophia danced around the benches. Some of Sophia's teachers from preschool came by and recognized Johnna and Sophia. One of our closest Starbucks workers passed by. Even our Covenant colleagues who live in the same town came by unexpectedly.

One of the homeless men joined in and played my guitar. He even spoke a few words in English, Spanish and French. As he played a song in Spanish, a Latino-Japanese woman stopped by, recognizing the song, and talked to me in Spanish. She loved to see Sophia dancing with such joy. Two teenage girls were watching us from a certain distance. Later, when we were ready to go catch our train inside the station, we saw them again. They ran toward us with a small gift for Sophia. Gift? Yes! We could not believe they were looking for us to give Sophia a gift. This is how our first Christmas ended in Japan after inexplicable encounters, very nice connections and a sweet divine touch.

Serving the Community as Bridges

A few months ago, Gabriel, the Brazilian-Japanese pastor came to me and said:

"Fábio, I am partnering with a non-profit organization in Nepal. They have projects against human trafficking."

"Tough work," I said.

"Yes, it is tough. I wonder if you could help me. One of the girls who came off the streets is a good singer. We have recorded an amateur album with a few songs. I wonder if you know someone who could make these songs into a CD. I would love to have some resources to help this project financially and I believe this could be one of the instruments to raise some funds for their organization."

A few weeks ago, Gabriel traveled to Brazil. I was able to connect him to a friend who has a recording studio. They got together and the CD project has already begun. Two other friends are also involved in the project. One close friend of mine is covering the costs of the production and the other one is developing the music background for each track. In addition, while they were in Brazil, pastor Gabriel and his family had an opportunity to meet my family in person. I am still looking for an answer as to why and how we have been experiencing so many connections, getting to know people much better than we expected and observing their vulnerability and availability to share their lives with us. We are amazed how often people in Japan ask us questions as we share our journeys in a country that is considered to be so daunting for

Christians organizations and missionaries since less than 1% are professing Christians and there are not more than 8,000 churches in the entire country. Maybe the answer is our sincere interest in learning Japanese, which helps us to connect to them. Maybe the answer is our intentionality to immerse ourselves in this vast ocean of language and culture, sometimes provoking admiration from native speakers because they see it as courageous. Maybe our backgrounds of travel and language study help us to connect to Japanese and other international people with ease. Maybe the answer is everything above in addition to the fact that it is crucial to discern and understand God's timing for each one of us. The ancient Greeks had two words for time, *chronos* and *kairos*. *Chronos* is referring to time that is orderly or chronological. In the New Testament we find out *kairos* means "the appointed time in the purpose of God."

It's possible that our multi-cultural and traveling experiences, our love for people, enthusiasm and sincere desire to learn all help us in some way, but overall, it is definitely God's timing that is behind what are experiencing as a dream - getting to serve different people, getting to know different cultures and sharing with so many families the meaning of the simple and pure Gospel.

Serving the Community

One of our activities to serve the community was to join eight others from three different churches (Japanese, Brazilian-Japanese and Latino-Japanese) to go to Kesennuma, one of the cities hit tragically by the 2011 tsunami. We drove eight hours during the night, arrived on a Saturday morning, and visited a Japanese church there that had been rebuilt with funds from Korean churches and others. From there, we went to the temporary housing area that hundreds have been living in after 100 days in their first building, a junior high school. The temporary housing area has a community center where we gathered. We pulled in with two already-cooked 24-pound turkeys, salad, rice, and pound cake for dessert. Thirty people showed up for a Christmas service with music in English and Japanese, a play telling the true meaning of Christmas, and a sermon followed by a meal that surprised everyone since most had never seen a turkey. Stories were told of how the town only lost people to the tsunami because those people chose to ignore the warning bells and either stayed or returned to their homes in unsafe conditions. We were moved by the group's strength, their smiles, and their generosity as a couple women kept showering Sophia with homemade jewelry and toys. Most of all, we were incredibly encouraged to be part of three churches of very different cultures working together to show the tsunami survivors that they are not forgotten. We could sense the meaning of this visit was to show how serving others really is equivalent to serving Jesus. We have learned to use a website called meetup.com to announce our activities. Currently, we run 7 groups like this one. Kamakura International Cafe is held at our Argentinian friends' cafe in a rather touristy town:

A Brazilian who lived in São Paulo, Toronto, Barcelona and Clearwater (Florida) and a North American who lived in Chicago, Isesaki (Gunma), Waterloo (Belgium) and Clearwater would like to ask you… Do you love to travel? Do you like to learn languages? We enjoy practicing Portuguese, English, French, Italian, Spanish and Japanese and are always looking for people to join us. We meet at Marion Crepes, Kamakura, on the 2nd and 4th Fridays of every month from 1pm-2pm. Estás listo para practicar tu español?? Você gosta de falar em Português? Va bene! Parliamo in Italiano! Ça va aller?!

言語が好きですか？ 英語、フランス語、スペイン語, 日本語、ポルトガル語, イタリア語?
君に会うのを楽しみに待っています ！

We are almost at the end of this chapter, but I do not want to miss the opportunity to share one of Johnna's emails to a friend in Santa Barbara, California. Here it is:

Some days we see impact more than others, but in the last 24 hours, I've counseled a young woman who is interested in missions, we have together counseled a teen who recently found out his girlfriend was pregnant, Fábio has been connecting a Brazilian soccer player and his wife to Japanese lessons and a local church, and we both had a meaningful conversation with one of my best Japanese friends about what we do here. She was confused as most people are at first, but her face lit up many times during the conversation and she said, "But that's so amazing you both enjoy doing the same things!" I was able to encourage her telling her the many ways she has also been a "bridge builder" in my life helping me with things that seem mundane to her like how to throw out garbage, where to find the stickers that go on the items to be thrown out, recording a Japanese TV show that we were on for us, telling me where to get Sophia's training pants and on and on. She couldn't believe it! Jesus is at work in Japan and Santa Barbara and around the world! May we all have eyes to see and join Jesus in the work he is about! I want to end this chapter by sharing what Johnna wrote in our newsletter of May 2016 because it expresses our prayers, our philosophy of ministry, and how we observe Japan, this beautiful country of impressive and beloved culture that is filled with friendly, hospitable people.

"Let me give you a new command: Love one another. In the same way I loved you, you love one another. This is how everyone will recognize that you are my disciples—when they see the love you have for each other" (John 13:34-35).

What would it look like to love freely, without trying to control, change or manipulate the other person? We don't always do it well, but that is one of the main tenets of our international and language groups, career coaching, resourcing, and even the way we strive to structure our marriage and parenting style. Jesus didn't heal everyone he met, he stepped away for long periods of time to be alone, he didn't always do what society expected of him, and he allowed people to be who they were around him without rules and expectations or following the status quo. I imagine it was his ability to allow people to be themselves, to speak truth without being judgmental, that brought the prostitutes, tax collectors, those on the margins of society, to him in droves.

People often ask us if we are trying to connect the people we meet to churches. The short answer is honestly, "no." Of course, if they have interest in visiting a church, we are thrilled to point them to a place that might be a good fit. We partner with several churches in teaching, preaching, counseling, empowering/resourcing, cross-cultural education and outreach. But most of the people we spend time with during the week have no interest in church (understood as a building where people meet weekly, distinguished from the Church that is an assembly or body of believers). Most of the people we get to see each week have never even met someone who tries to follow the teachings of Jesus.

They're agnostics and atheists, Buddhists, Hindus and Confucianists. They can talk about science, music, philosophy, and religion. All of the people we spend time with have a hunger to see love in action. When people are introduced to the historical Jesus through his own words, often they can see his teachings clearly, without needing to undo layers of religion, rules and hypocrisy. And this is how they know who Jesus' disciples are - they see them loving each other and experience love in action from them. May we somehow be conduits of this love to one another and to those around us!

Chapter 9

Jesus is not the Founder of Christianity

"I saw no temple in the city, for its temple is the Lord God the Almighty and the Lamb."
Apostle John (Revelation 21:22)

For My Atheist Friends (Christians, don't get mad)

Jesus is not the founder of Christianity. Why is this so important? What does it have to do with our mission and spiritual journey? How can I explain to my friends for whom Jesus is the first image they have in mind when they hear the word Christianity? In the last ten years, at least once a week, without exaggeration I meet someone with whom I talk about this subject. In fact, as soon as I'm able to clarify this difference, a common ground is established and we can talk about the historical Jesus, his life and teachings without the shadow and ghosts of Christianity as a religious and historical phenomenon. The fact is, it is much easier to explain this difference between the Jesus of the Gospel narratives and the Christian religious perspective to a non-church person than to a church person.

Why can't church people see the difference? Why are some

Christians even afraid to disagree with their leaders, pastors, priests or denominations when they find something that doesn't match between the way Jesus lived and what they are experiencing at their church? Why are Christians more apt to follow a certain leader, religious movement or denomination than to follow Jesus Christ himself? These are important questions that I've been asking myself for the last few years. So, why do church people struggle to understand what is clear, simple and obvious?

It seems to me that most of the church people I have known for thirty years cannot see God outside of Sunday school or the church walls. They know what they know about Jesus from the message they hear from the pulpits. Church has become a "club." Being a Christian is just a label. They keep having countless struggles, some live a double life, but they keep their Christian label untouched, going so far as to fight against any political or moral issue that might threaten the Christian faith.

It is very sad that there is nothing new here. Anyone who reads a bit of history will see that our Western world was Christianized. I haven't taken any history classes since high school and college, but each one of us has heard and read about the Christian influence in Western colonization. We have seen how "Christian" nations, Catholic or Protestant, such as Spain, Portugal, France, Netherlands and England have been like gladiators in the area of colonized territories. We have seen Christian influence in economical, political and social events throughout Western history for centuries. It is no coincidence that Mahatma Gandhi, when observing the oppression of the population of India by the British Empire said to the British soldiers: "I like your Christ, but I do not like you Christians. You Christians are so unlike your Christ."[47] If Jesus got dressed in blood and flesh to show the image of a loving and merciful God to teach everyone how humankind should behave, we have no alternative but to ask ourselves a few honest questions.

Why don't we see the results of true Christianity in our Western society after 2,000 years? Why have we become more cynical,

---

[47] For more, see http://www.goodreads.com/quotes/22155-i-like-your-christ-i-do-not-like-your-christians.

selfish, individualistic, even living out the antitheses of Jesus' teaching from generation to generation? Why so very often do Christians seem to live so far from the simplicity of Jesus's lifestyle? Why has the world become a post-Christian society that is tired of all the Christian talk? If Jesus is not the founder of Christianity as I propose, then who is?

Christianity has a founder, but the founder is not Jesus. Jesus didn't come to create any religion, new political movement or philosophical thought to compete with the Greeks. Jesus did not have anything to do with any religious group in Palestine in the 1st Century. He was not a Pharisee who could be compared to today's "right" political and ideological parties. He was not a Sadducee that played a more central political role those days. Some people have said that Jesus could have been an Essene. The Essenes lived in the desert, far away from Jewish society. They practiced ways of asceticism, therefore we know Jesus was not an Essene. He was not a Zealot either because Zealots had a leftist ideological and political view. And last, Jesus had nothing to do with the Sicarii, a splinter group of the Hebrew Zealots that became a "terrorist group" by having extreme leftist ideological and political ideas. Jesus did not have any partisanship with any political movement at all.

The Roman Emperor Constantine founded Christianity in the 4th Century in 332 AD. Christianity is a group of systemized doctrines (this is what "ism" means in Greek) like any other "ism": Judaism, Buddhism, Hinduism, etc. Once again, I remind you the importance of the book *The Subversion of Christianity* by Jacques Ellul. It is an extraordinary document and important book for anyone who wants to understand how Christianity has built more walls than bridges between people and cultures over the centuries.

Have you ever taken a look at a historical event regarding Christianity? Have you ever taken Jesus out of the political and religious Christianity package? Have you ever tried to match Jesus' teachings with what Christianity has been representing for centuries in history? Have you ever tried to have a conversation with your friends by showing this difference and presenting Jesus from the Gospels? If you have not done this exercise, I can affirm that most people, if not all, in Europe, North and South America, and Asia, with whom I've had the opportunity to talk about my faith and spiritual journey had a very simple equation: Jesus equals

98

Christianity, therefore, Christianity equals Jesus. But the truth is, though Christianity has a lot of Jesus influence, Jesus is not the equivalent of Christianity.

John Stott, one of the most influential theologians of the 20th Century, taught us and emphasized in his last book, *The Radical Disciple*,[48] that not every Christian is a disciple of Jesus, but every disciple of Jesus is a Christian. The disciples of Jesus were called Christians for the first time in Acts: "The disciples were called Christians first at Antioch" (Acts 11:26b). They were called Christians because they followed the Christ, not the religious phenomenon created later by Constantine in the 4th Century. The truth is that the world will know us not because we have a label called Christian, but because we love each other. "By this everyone will know that you are my disciples, if you love one another," (John 13:35). The truth is that the world expects honesty, transparency, compassion, sincerity, a life without judgmental statements and a life without hypocrisy from those who assume a genuine and authentic Christian identity.

Genuine and authentic Christian identity, what does it mean? Yes, indeed, I'm talking about Christian identity as followers of Christ and not christian (little "c") identity as just a part of a certain religious group. Christian identity means we are Christians because we follow the Christ, live like him, love like him, respond to life like Him, care for justice like Him, embrace the cause of the poor and marginalized people like Him, and it does *not* mean christians just as members of the religious movement of Christianity that benefits us socially and politically.

How could we compare Jesus to the Christian movement in history? Where should we start? How can we get close enough to our friends, colleagues and families in order to have a conversation about Jesus and his historicity? How often do we meet individuals who connect Jesus with the current political situations in the United States and Latin America where evangelical politics are claimed to

---

[48] *The Radical Disciple*, Published in the United States of America by InterVarsity Press, Downers Grove, Illinois, with permission from Inter-Varsity Press, England.

be the christian "role", but at the same time support wars, segregation, are against Muslim communities and anyone or anything that could threaten our "christian" ideologies?

Is Everything About Christianity Bad? Isn't There Anything Good?

It is not hard to see once we go back a few chapters in history that there were bloody wars on behalf of God, long crusades, insane inquisitions, selfish political-economical-religious interests behind the indulgences, battles between religion and science, power and ambition, promiscuity among popes, darkness in the middle ages, sexual repression and imposed moralism for centuries on behalf of a false devotion to a powerful religion that always compromised the values of Jesus in order to have political status regardless of the type of government in charge at any given moment. It didn't matter if the platform of power was made up of monarchies, democracies, nazis, dictatorships or any other political model. The church as a political institution has always tried to work next to the State. In short, history is a continuous repetition of past events. The fact is that God is not the exclusive property of any religion. No group or movement has a patent on God. No one owns God. God is God. What else do we need to add? Does it make any sense to box God in a bunch of doctrines and systematic rules? God is love, and here we could end our questions and answers, but let's continue. What does love mean? How did Jesus live his life? Is Jesus my standard to understand and interpret everything? How much have I come to know Jesus and his attitudes through the Gospel narratives? "God is spirit, and those who worship him must worship in spirit and truth" (John 4:24).

I know you may have a few questions in your mind right now. One of them could be: "Fábio, do you believe that there has been anything good in Christianity as a religious movement?" Yes, my answer is positive. Yes! Certainly, we have had a few sparkles in history where someone here and a movement there tried to bring back the simplicity of Jesus' teachings. Examples are John Wycliffe in the 14th Century and William Tyndale in the 15th Century among others who have been inspiring me and millions of people over the centuries. John Wesley in the 18th Century made an expressive social impact in his days, after being kicked out of the Church of England that represented a political and powerful institution. He brought a genuine revival and powerful holistic message to his generation.

In Europe, nearly five hundred years later, we cannot ignore the fact that Martin Luther and Calvin started a new historical chapter in the 16th Century. A German monk, Luther protested the selling of indulgences to escape purgatory and other practices of the medieval Roman Catholic Church. Luther also affirmed that God's Word, not the word of any pope or council, should be more relevant than the Scriptures. Three phrases shaped the Reformation theology: sola fide (faith alone), sola gratia (grace alone) and sola scriptura (Scripture alone). Luther insisted that anyone could be justified by faith through what God did in Christ. Therefore, it was Jesus who did all the work; no one was, is or will be able to be justified by intellectual or creedal acquiescence. God's salvation is a gift. It is given by grace. As humans we do not merit this gift.

Luther nailed his ninety-five theses to the door of All Saints' Church in Wittenberg on October 31, 1517. This was a crucial moment for the Reformation. After almost 1200 years of people not having access to the Bible because it was imprisoned and interpreted only by cardinals and popes (the pseudo-authorized "representatives of God"), Luther and Calvin along with Tyndale and Wycliffe are to be remembered for creating the first translations of the Bible in English, German and French. Finally, the Scriptures were made available to everyone. Nevertheless, in spite of their good intentions, all was not perfect. For example, Luther could not avoid getting involved in the German Peasants' War. Though he took a middle course, he wasn't able to keep the war from happening. Even the best version of historical Christianity has brought political implications. If we keep reading and studying meticulously about the Reformation, we will come across countless conflicts and battles from the Thirty Years' War in Europe until the most recent revolts between Catholics and Protestants in Northern Ireland.

In fact, political and personal interests have frequently taken over spiritual initiatives and the results have been a terrible disaster. In the 16th Century, John Calvin was an absolutely brilliant theologian. His commentaries on biblical books, his influence in the Western world and his main work, *The Institutes of the Christian Religion,*[49] have been appreciated by millions of people for centuries. But even Calvin tainted his reputation when Michael Servetus was burned at the stake as a heretic in Geneva by order of the city's Protestant governing council presided by him. This incident is still mourned among both Presbyterians and Calvinists today. Calvin found that he had little choice but to ask the civil authorities to intervene. Historian Francis Higman says, "There was a sort of horrid inevitability about the whole thing." Calvin had no political authority whatsoever, and was not even a citizen of Geneva until six years later. Calvin did what he could, which was to ask the civil authorities to investigate the matter and to take action. They consulted churches in Geneva and elsewhere in Switzerland and found that this was a matter worthy of trial. The trial was lengthy and deliberate. Servetus was eventually found guilty and was condemned to be burned at the stake, despite Calvin's request that he be executed painlessly by beheading. Michael Servetus was put to death on October 27, 1553. Several months later the Catholic Inquisition in France executed him once more, this time in effigy.[50]

Unfortunately, after an attempt by the Reformers to get back to the simplicity of Jesus' message without hierarchy and religious ambition, theologians started getting together to debate the Scriptures while losing sight of the main proposals of the Reformation. In other words, it was the beginning of intellectualism and scholasticism in Europe. A new glimpse and sparkle of hope was born through the Pietist movement and then, Philipp Jakob Spener, August Hermann Francke and other Pietists rose up to guide European awareness back to the principles of the Reformation and above all things, to the genuine call of a truly Christian life. *Pia Desideria,*[51] written by Spener, became an extremely important

---

[49]See http://www.ccel.org/ccel/calvin/institutes/

[50] See (http://www.challies.com/articles/the-servetus-problem)

[51] I heard about Pia Desideria at my first meeting for Covenant World Mission in 2015. I absolutely recommend this book, especially for those who love church

document in those days, the classic statement of Pietism. This was the birth of small groups of prayer, Bible study, learning, mutual encouragement and what they called "conventicles." It became a movement against the state church. However, we do not always see the effects of this movement in modern times. For example, when I start talking to people about faith and Christianity, Jesus and my own journey, eventually, a topic like science comes up. It is almost pathetic when we get to Galileo Galilei's issue and admit that the Vatican didn't apologize until 350 years after Galileo's Inquisition process. It is almost pathetic to have to admit that Christianity has had popes like Alexander VI, one of the most controversial popes of the Renaissance period, who served as inspiration for Machiavelli's "The Prince." The book was centered on Cesare Borgia, the illegitimate son of Pope Alexander, and his quest for power, from whom Machiavelli drew his philosophical concepts.

Jesus and Christianity - Most People Can't Separate Them

It is sad and horrible to realize we are connected to this reputation of Christianity the minute we assume our identity as a disciple of Jesus, but at the same time, the negative image of historical Christianity can become an opportunity to deconstruct the concept of Jesus as founder of a religion. In fact, after talking to anyone openly and honestly about the above examples, current evangelical political ideologies that have nothing to do with the simplicity of Jesus' teachings, we end up asking questions such as: Where is Jesus in all these things we are talking about? Have you ever read what Jesus teaches in the Gospels? Have you only ever heard about Jesus from your christian friends, evangelical programs on TV or relatives? Do you really think Jesus has to do with these political events?

If we look for inspiring sparkles and a glimpse of hope in

history. See a short summary of Philip Jacob Spener's book at http://www.christianitytoday.com/history/issues/issue-10/from-archives-pia-desideria-pious-desires.html

America in the 18th and 19th Centuries, we must acknowledge the powerful and positive influence of Charles Finney and Jonathan Edwards and later, D.L. Moody. I would even add our contemporary brother, Billy Graham. However, we cannot deny the horrible Salem witch trials in Massachusetts between February 1692 and May 1693. I am making a superficial historical line by evoking a few names, historical movements and examples that come to mind as I write this chapter. I do not even need to mention the current evangelical fundamentalist politicians, mega churches, prosperity theology and evangelical ideologies that have been significantly present in Africa, all of Latin America, and the United States. They have been subjects of my talks with every single non-church person I meet. We need not be surprised that the world is watching us, this "christian" movement, to see what happens as we take up political positions, make decisions and opine about any social matter, but especially, they are watching to see how we respond to daily life. Luther said, "How come Christ traveled on foot, but the pope in a palanquin with a retinue of three or four thousand mule drivers; how come Christ washed the feet of sinners but the pope has them kiss his toes?"[52]

Five centuries after Luther's reflection, today I could say the same: How come Christ was born in a manger and pastors and leaders of the church drive expensive cars and stay in 5-star hotels? How come Jesus avoided being made king by the multitudes while our pastors and church leaders crave the spotlight and marketing strategies that will keep them in the center of attention? How come Jesus did not avoid marginalized or excluded groups of people, but we create apartheid and segregation because of religion, skin color and economic class? The genuine, authentic and true Church has always been a group of people who walked away from the political system, individualistic and selfish ideologies, and ambition for power, money and status. They have been followers of Christ by spreading the good news of Jesus in love by God's grace through faith. They have been persecuted. They have been killed. They never compromise His values. They have been salt and light of the world.

---

[52] Eschatology and Ethics: Essays on the Theology and Ethics of the Kingdom of God by Carl E. Braaten, p.80.

They have been the reflection of Jesus, their Master and Lord.

Are You a Disciple of Jesus or a Disciple of Christianity?

Why do so many of us struggle to live out our faith as disciples of Jesus in a post-Christian society? Why do most of us know nothing or almost nothing of historical Christianity? Why do most Christians get offended when Christianity is compared to other religions that have done atrocities on behalf of God? The truth is as long as we keep connecting Jesus to Christianity, we will have less and less capacity to testify about Jesus and his life in a post-Christian world. We need to be honest followers of Jesus, understanding our identity as children of God, not children of Christianity.

Unfortunately, the reputation of a Protestant, Christian or Evangelical has changed dramatically. In the past, being a Protestant was a sign of being honest, having good ethics and integrity in Europe. The word evangelical comes from the Greek word related to the gospel, or good news. The term is also used to refer to Christians and comes from the same root. This terminology has been damaged these last decades. Frequently, when I am asked if I am Christian, Evangelical or Protestant, my answer is, "Well, it depends on how you define those terms."

The good news is when we take any person from any background through the long, but necessary process of explaining the post-Christian world, the misunderstood and damaged concepts of Christian, Evangelical and Protestant, the influence of globalization and then, with patience and knowledge are willing to show them the difference between the Jesus of the religion Christianity and the Jesus of the Gospels, we will be able to put them face to face with the most fascinating personality this world has ever seen. The Gospel narratives become the main resource to present Jesus and what he came to do 2,000 years ago. Jesus is able to introduce himself through his own words. It is a slow process. We should remove the layers of religiosity one by one as we answer question after question and go deeper and deeper in conversation displaying honesty and comprehension as we talk about these complex and delicate subjects. It's similar to peeling an onion, layer by layer.

Sometimes, it feels like we will never reach the core.

We live in a crucial moment of time where, more than ever, we meet people who are burned out on religion. People who may not believe in anything due to a certain negative experience in their own families, a local institutional church, or just because they simply observe historical facts and conclude: If this is what they call God, I want nothing to do with Him. As we meet new people, developing friendships naturally, we can create opportunities, connections, links, clarify concepts, and share our own spiritual journey in order to turn our talks toward Jesus and his historical life without imposing anything, but just as revealing part of our being, our DNA.

What experiences have you had when you meet new people? Am I the only one who meets people who are tired of religious talk? Am I the only one who gets a reproving look if I say the name Jesus or talk about the church, Christianity or anything related to the Christian life? Often I meet people who grew up in a pastor's home where their father or mother could speak about love from the pulpit easily. However, the same lovely person from the pulpit does not respect anyone as soon as he is back home. I meet a businessman whose grandparents were missionaries. He grew up under fear and panic. If he did not accept Jesus and go to church, he would go to hell.

I meet many people who are burned out on religion due to manipulation on different levels or an abusive behavior on behalf of God. They become atheists or agnostics and build up a huge resistance toward God and God's love. You may be thinking: "Fábio, I understand and agree with you, but I understand that this is reality in the Western world. I also have friends who have had bad experiences in churches or something related to this type of Christianity you have been describing, but Japan must be different. It does not have the residual damage from the political power of Christianity as an institutional organization from the Western perspective."

I agree, but I also have a "but." The fact is, as mentioned before, whenever I meet someone, it always seems necessary to walk the institutional path of separating Jesus of the Gospel from the atrocities in history made on behalf of a certain "Christian God." Always! Before our talk, they are already aware of the historical facts and have a fixed concept in their mind: Christianity is only a

Western religion, therefore, it has nothing to do with me. Therefore, my ultimate goal is to take a person from any background, culture or experience and encourage her or him to read who Jesus is according to Matthew, Mark, Luke and John. This includes my time in Japan or when I talk to any non-Western person in any part of the world. As I begin sharing the principles that Jesus taught such as "Do to others what you would like them to do to you and love your enemy and pray for those who persecute you" and point to the Gospel to be our main historical source, things start to go in a different direction. As I keep challenging each one to meet the historical Jesus in the Gospel narratives, inviting them to read the descriptions and historical facts as they would read any newspaper or magazine, the misconception of Christianity and the Western religion barrier no longer exist between us.

What does it mean to be a "disciple of Jesus?"

At this point in our journey, I believe it's important to clarify that to be a disciple of Jesus is not the same as what it means for many when they hear the word "christian." To be a disciple of Jesus means to do His will and act like Him. "You are Israel's teacher," said Jesus, "and do you not understand these things?" Jesus said to Nicodemus when the topic was being born again. It is not about our hermeneutic. It is not about our exegesis. It is not about our moralism. It is not about our group of doctrines or religious heritage. It is about Jesus, his life and His main message that is found in the Sermon of the Mount that has to do with love, compassion, justice, inclusion, and forgiveness, calling us to be peacemakers full of mercy.

John summarizes this simple message, "Let us love one another, for love is of God; and everyone who loves is born of God and knows God" (1 John 4:7). Do you love? Do I love? Do we see life and every human being through the lenses of love and compassion with the same spirit that Jesus has? If yes, we know God and we were genuinely born again. Or, I don't love? We don't see life and every human being through lenses of love and compassion with the same spirit Jesus has? The answer is "a sincere no, I do not." We do not. You and I do not know God, we just know religious doctrines, moral rules, attend a place called church and have been catechized to belong to a social-religious group.

"Hi, my name is Kikuda. Nice to meet you!" a young Japanese man introduced himself in very good Portuguese at my first Portuguese group conversation in Fujisawa.

"'Nice to meet you." I responded. "Welcome!"

I could not believe how well Kikuda spoke Portuguese. He was not a nikkei, second generation Japanese. He was totally Japanese! It was just the beginning of one more conversation that would lead me to share about my faith in Jesus. I got even more surprised when he asked me a few more questions during the conversation group.

"How did you come to Japan? What kind of visa do you have?" he asked.

"Religious visa," I answered, thinking it was strange because no one had ever asked me that question.

"Are you a pastor?" he continued with the questions.

"Yes, I am."

"Are you a christian?" he asked, curiously waiting for my answer.

"Well, it depends on your definition of christian," I replied.

To make a long story short, when the conversation group ended, I spent the next hour answering more of his questions until I finally told him I had to go back home. It turns out Kikuda had a few experiences with some Brazilians in Japan. Unfortunately, those Brazilians belonged to a certain Pentecostal group that has brought a lot of syncretism to the evangelical Brazilian movement by aggressively preaching prosperity theology. It is not the first time that I met someone like Kikuda. I am sure you know people like him. I met several people like him in Europe, in the USA, and now in Japan. I will not be surprised if these types of encounters increase going forward since the message of Jesus, the cross, the simplicity of the Gospel, has been diluted in most parts of the planet. Kikuda came back a different day to ask me more questions. One time, I arrived early and he was there, too, ready to talk to me before class.

"I cannot understand you. You say what you say, but you affirm that you are not a religious person," he said.

"You are right. I am not. Religions tend to manipulate - taking away a person's right to think for himself - deceive the poor, ignorant and needy, and take advantage of political power." I could see his curiosity was piqued.

"Well, the Bible is the only book that I don't recommend reading from beginning to end. If you don't know about Jesus, you might not be able to read the Old Testament through the message of the New Testament," I started explaining to him. "Most of the Old Testament themes are appointed to Jesus. They are merely shadows of events that would happen in the future. Instead, I recommend that you read Matthew, Mark, Luke and John just as you would read the newspaper. Then, you will find out how Jesus treated women, how he spoke to people considered "sinners", how he condemned religiosity, hypocrisy and any false type of spirituality." As soon as I completed my last words, I could see he was intrigued by my answer.

"Jesus did not ask anyone to follow Catholicism, Protestantism or any kind of religion," I continued.

"I have never heard anyone talking like this," he said. "You are right," he continued. "Jesus never asked anyone to follow one of those religions," he smiled at me. Finally, after our conversation, I knew I could bring a Japanese New Testament for him the next time I saw him.

"Kikuda, now it is my turn to ask you questions. Let me ask you two things," I said as I held the New Testament in my hands.

"Sure! No problem," he smiled while waiting for my questions.

"Have you ever heard of capitalism? Do you know how to define it?" I asked him.

"Yes, of course. Capitalism is an economic system where people buy and sell products freely," he defined it.

"Have you ever heard of Adam Smith or read anything by him?"

"No, I have not."

"Well, he is the father of capitalism. Do you think there is a difference between hearing about capitalism through a book or other people and getting the information directly from the main source?" I asked him.

"Yes, of course. I know what you mean," he answered me already knowing where I was taking him.

"It is like going to Barcelona or Singapore. You have heard about them, but when you go there yourself, your conclusions change. Or it's like an apple. I can describe an apple to you: red, round, a delicious taste. Some people try it and like it, some do not. But, there is only one way to decide if you like it or not - you must try it." I finished my thought as I kept looking at the New Testament.

When I finished, I encouraged him to read the book of John to learn everything about the historical Jesus. Also, I told him with a smile not to come back with any other questions until he had finished his readings and "homework." Jesus is so fascinating that every popular religion has included him in its portfolio in one way or another. He has been considered the most illuminated spirit of light, a great prophet, one of the divine incarnations, even a respectful person we all should read about.

After all, Who IS Jesus according to the Gospels?

In the Gospels, Jesus hangs out with sinners and tax collectors. Jesus very often accepts invitations to have dinner with those who are marginalized. Jesus feasts constantly and the religious people get jealous and do not understand him. They persecute him. They follow him when he goes north of Israel. They send a group of religious spies to see if he goes south after going north. They go everywhere he goes and ask him questions to find a way to incriminate him. They do this with intentionality, waiting for the right moment to kill him. After the resurrection of Lazarus, this is what John writes quoting the chief priests and Pharisees: "Here is this man performing many signs. If we let him go on like this, everyone will believe in him, and then the Romans will come and take away both our temple and our nation," (John 11:47-48).

Religious groups judged Jesus and said, "He's a glutton and a drunkard, and a friend of tax collectors and other sinners," (Matthew 11:19). Jesus did not reject anyone, rather he included everyone. His parables give multiple examples of how we should live life and how God sees our attitude and behavior. In Luke, Chapter 15, he talks about the audience and public that were drawn to Jesus' audience. He says, "Now the tax collectors and sinners were all gathering around to hear Jesus. But the Pharisees and the teachers of the law muttered, 'This man welcomes sinners and eats with them'" (Luke 15:1-2).

When I read Jesus in the Gospel and observe his parables, my questions are: Who am I? Who are you? Who have we been? Are we like the tax collectors, sinners and prostitutes with gratitude in our hearts for receiving Jesus' forgiveness and acceptance in love? Are we like Jesus, acting like Jesus, living life like Jesus? Receiving those that no one wants to receive? Embracing the causes of those that no one wants to embrace? Or have we been like the religious groups, acting with arrogance and superiority, full of certainty and better than everybody else because of our correct behavior and moralism?

Jesus in Islam - Did you know that the Quran puts Jesus higher than Muhammad? So, Why Don't Muslims Believe and Follow Jesus?

Jesus fascinates people with any type of background, past, experience, language or culture. When we take anyone on the path of the historical Jesus as told from the Gospels, he or she gets amazed by reading and reflecting on the life of Jesus. A Brazilian like me (not "nikkei," not second generation) came to our second International Hangout. Carlos lived in Ireland. He was studying a PhD program in one of the universities in town. Nice guy and very intelligent. After a few meetings we got together alone to have some coffee. That afternoon, while I was waiting for him, I read my Quran because I've been studying Muslim culture and Islam for two years and finally bought a Quran in Portuguese to go deeper.

"Hey, what are you reading there?" he asked me as soon as he saw me.

"This is the Quran, I answered him as I started putting it in my backpack."

"Are you allowed to read it?" he asked me with a surprised look on his face.

"Why not?" I answered.

That first conversation was the first one of many we would have about Buddhism, Jesus, science, Christianity, mega evangelical churches, evangelical politicians, popes, the Protestant Reformation and much more. These hours of conversation made us good friends. On a different occasion, we discussed how religion, power and politics have walked together in history. Nothing different or new from what I have been writing down on these pages.

"What have you learned by reading the Quran?" he asked me.

"Do you know the Quran says that Jesus was born of a virgin? Muhammad was not. Do you know the Quran says that Jesus did miracles? Muhammad didn't do any miracles. Do you know the Quran says that Jesus was the Anointed One, the Christ of God? Muhammad was not. Jesus will come again according to the Quran. Muhammad died and is buried in Medina in western Saudi Arabia," I said. Little by little we began to trust each other more.

"If Islam says these things about Jesus, why do they not follow Jesus?" he asked me.

"Good question," I replied. "Number one, when some Muslims find out what I just described, they go to the Gospel narratives in order to learn about Jesus and how he lived historically."

"Really?"

"Yes. As a result of that, many of them become disciples of Jesus, or disciples of Isa, the name of Jesus in Arabic. Number two, many others do not want to give this credit to Jesus even though the Quran puts Jesus on a higher level than Muhammad. Do you know why?"

"Why?" he asked curiously, waiting for the answer.

"Because of the tragic historical conflict between Christianity and Islam."

That afternoon we had a deep, open and honest talk about how the power of religion overshadows the beauty of Jesus' life and his simplicity. Carlos told me he would like to keep talking to me about these subjects. He also expressed his interest in knowing more about the historical Jesus. Later, we got together again and this time, I had a Bible to give him. I suggested he read the Gospels before anything else in order to understand the life of Jesus, who he was, what he said and how he taught. Before Carlos went back to Brazil, he introduced his parents to me. They came to see where he lived in Japan and had a chance to spend some days with him traveling in Asia. As I drove them to the train station in a downpour that cold night, he started his "thankful speech" for everything Johnna and I had done for him and other people like him who did not have their families in Japan. Before he left my car, we hugged each other a few times with tears in our eyes, and then, he expressed his gratitude for our meetings, talks and example as a family. I thanked him for his honesty, friendship and hours of talks and conversations. Since his return to Brazil, we have kept in touch, getting even closer and continuing the conversations we started about anything and everything through Skype. We have become "digital friends" out of necessity.

De-religiofy Jesus: Everyone Around Us Is Sick and Tired of Christian Talk

More and more lately, I've been realizing that in every encounter, every talk with every person I meet, my mission is to do a process that I have been calling the "de-religiofication" of Jesus. Yes! I mean that once I take Jesus out of any religious package, "de-religiofying" him, and start explaining historical facts by demystifying concepts regarding Christianity, I replace those ideas with the real Jesus of the Gospels and a different atmosphere is created. In fact, what I have been noticing is the importance of letting people know me as part of this journey: how I respond to daily life, how I treat my daughter, how Johnna and I are able to stay together even though we may have different points of view on certain subjects, whether or not I make room to ask someone for forgiveness when I make mistakes, honor my parents, choose to respect my neighbors and interact with any other human being whether or not he or she shares the same cultural background, language or belief. In spite of Christianity and its historical, religious, and political heritage, I am convinced that God has been actively revealing Himself in any way He wants, to whomever He wants - to millions and millions of people on earth, unknown tribes, unique cultures. For this, I highly recommend the book *Eternity in Their Hearts*[53] written by the Canadian missionary and writer, Don Richardson. It is an important document that will help clarify what I am going to talk about in the next chapters. So, please stay with me and let's continue on our journey.

---

[53] *Eternity in Their Hearts* by Don Richardson, is a book for anyone interested in missiology. Bethany House edition published 2014. Previously published by Regal Books. First Edition 1981, Second Edition 1984, Third Edition 2005.

Chapter 10

How to Discern and Hear God's Voice

"So, as the Holy Spirit says: Today, if you hear his voice,
do not harden your hearts"
Hebrews 3:7-8a

For My Agnostic Friends

These may be the most intriguing human questions - Does God
exist? Who is God? How and where can we find God? How can we
hear and discern God's voice? Does God speak? And if there is a
God, an absolute powerful being, does He care for us? Well, we
should start with the fact that God is not an academic or theoretical
experience. God is not a subject to be studied meticulously in
scientific labs. God is infinitely bigger than what one can learn
during a few years of Bible college. God is immensely bigger than
our theological convictions and theological achievements whether
they be Masters of Divinity, PhDs in missiology or any other

religious matter.

With that in mind, we realize that unfortunately, very often, most of the people who spend years in theological studies, attending churches, mosques or temples, hours of meditation and religious studies, hours of practicing a life of asceticism among other religious practices, may become individuals who walk on an arrogant and presumptuous path by putting themselves in a superior place, assuming they are the ones who carry information that no one else knows. They are the ones who always have some kind of knowledge to offer. This is the most dangerous temptation that any religious group can have, namely, the presupposition of knowing God exclusively.

Let's go back to our "Christian world" conversation because it is what matters here. Sometimes our attempt at evangelization and mission becomes a complicated road, especially if we have decided to have a cross-cultural experience and think we are bringing God to a "pagan culture." They are aliens, we think. They need us. God isn't there yet, there's no Christian presence, so we will make the difference. We can change the environment. We will bring salvation, we are the answer. In other words, we come with a messianic complex. It is there, in our hearts, even though it may be unconscious or blurry, it is the message that abides our being. Instead, we need not forget the reality that God is already actively working in every square inch of the earth! God is already at work in every culture and has been working since the beginning. God has been working since the first civilization, the first era, the first human being, and will continue working until the last civilization, era and human being. If we know God, if we have been called to a specific mission, if God has a purpose and plan for our lives, my question is this: How much does my knowledge of God bring peace to my being? How much does my personal journey and experience with God calm my heart? Does my knowledge of God make me judge others, building walls between people and cultures, or does it purify my eyes to see life according to God's lenses? Does my experience and journey with God make me a better human being?

Our faith in Jesus should not make us feel superior to anyone, but rather, it's supposed to humble us and put us on the same level as others in order to serve, in love, whomever crosses our path, just as Jesus came to serve humankind. Our faith in Jesus should bring serenity to our hearts and make us aware of the fact that God's voice goes out through all the earth and His words to the end of the world (Psalm 19:4). For me, it's enough to know the privilege of being His cooperator. It is enough to know that I pursue my career and mission in life resting in His arms, knowing He is actively revealing Himself to whomever He wants. Any human, in any culture, anywhere, may be able to experience a glimpse of His unconditional love.

Although there are differences among Christian theologians, most will agree that God is self-existent, omnipresent, omnipotent, omniscient, the Creator of the universe, Eternal and Infinite, interacting with us, His creatures. He speaks to us. He loves us unconditionally. A simple and short summary would be that humans are called to glorify His name as we travel as pilgrims on the journey of life, under the sun, and also are called to enjoy and rejoice in Him eternally.

Where can we hear God's voice? How can we discern when God talks to us? Is there any specific place in which we need to be in order to find God? Basically, according to Christian theology, there are four main pillars through which God speaks to us: nature, our conscience, the Scriptures and Jesus. Most of us in the Western world have received historical information about Jesus such as where he was born and what he did and then, the divine revelation took place in our hearts. We decided to follow Jesus by recognizing that he is the Son of God, the Christ of God.

In reality, our veil fell off allowing us to see God in Christ, reconciling the world unto himself, not imputing their trespasses unto them (2 Corinthians 5:19). However, we should remind ourselves that there are no formulas when talking about things of God. God is not a group of doctrines. God is not Christianity or a religious historical phenomenon, or any religion, by the way. When we're talking about God, we're talking about the Creator of everything, the One who is able to be found when any person decides to seek Him with a sincere heart in spirit and truth. The One who is Eternal. The One who is Spirit, who knows hearts and secret thoughts. There is no manual to understand how God works. He is God. I am a simple man. He is divine. I am just a human being, He is absolute. If we cannot understand how our brain works or the multiple universes and galaxies that exist, if we cannot understand how our cells work, how can we pretend to say we understand how

God works? How can we define God in a meticulous fashion? We can't! How can we pretend to study God as a subject at universities and Bible colleges? As Paul wrote, let's join in a choir and say with him, "Oh, the depth of the riches of the wisdom and knowledge of God! How unsearchable his judgments, and his paths beyond tracing out! Who has known the mind of the Lord? Or who has been his counselor? Who has ever given to God, that God should repay them? For from him and through him and for him are all things. To him be the glory forever! Amen" (Romans 11:33-36).

When I travel the world, visiting cities, talking to new groups of people, studying different cultures and ancient civilizations, I ask myself, "Did these ancient civilizations ever hear about Jesus? How did they learn about him if no church, group of missionaries or Christian organization reached them in the distant regions of the globe? How did they experience God's salvation if they were not allowed to speak freely about the historical Christ?" If today, in the 21st Century, over 2,000 people groups do not have the New Testament in their mother languages (according to Wycliffe Association), how many people didn't have access to the Scriptures in their own language during the last five hundred years? If I think about the 16th Century before the Protestant Reformation, the Bible was only able to be read by Catholic priests, popes, bishops and scholars - how was God able to speak to the millions of people groups, tribes and villages that didn't have access?

I still remember when I was a teenager and I read Psalm 19:1-4, "The heavens are telling the glory of God; and the firmament proclaims his handiwork. Day to day pours forth speech, and night to night declares knowledge. There is no speech, nor are there words; their voice is not heard; yet their voice goes out through all the earth, and their words to the end of the world." Nature cannot point to me who God is, but it allows me to see His fingerprints everywhere. Nature cannot tell me who God is, but I am able to testify that there is something beyond the force of the sun, the immense and deep Pacific ocean, the vast and unspoken universe. Nature cannot guide me into God's lap, but at least I may be in awe of His majestic piece of art - His creation that astonishes all of his creatures.

When we lived in Clearwater, Florida, every Thursday I woke up between 5-5:30am and drove to Indian Rocks beach. When I got there, it was still dark. I always started walking on the beach and felt the cold between my toes. It was the only time I could feel cold sand in Florida. As I stayed on the beach for a moment of solitude, the sunrise there was one of the most amazing things I have ever experienced. As I observed the transition from darkness to light, there was not one time that I didn't think about what the apostle Paul wrote to the Romans. "For what can be known about God is plain to them, because God has shown it to them. Ever since the creation of the world his eternal power and divine nature, invisible though they are, have been understood and seen through the things he has made. So they are without excuse" (Romans 1:19-20).

The Immanence and Transcendence of God

This is exactly what we call the immanence of God. God is in the sun, but the sun is not God. God is in the dense smell of the forests, but the forests are not God. God is in the deep and wild sound of the waves and seas, but the waves and seas are not God. God is seen in everything that He has made and created, but "everything" is not God, because He transcends His creation. His creation is not an extensive part of His being. God is outside space and time. God's transcendence tells me He is not created. You and I exist because we have a beginning and an end on this earth. Did God make God? Who created God? No one! If He were a created being, the presupposition would be someone somewhere made God, but He is self-existent, therefore, God IS. At this point of our journey, we have walked a long way to be aware of the fact that God is much bigger than our human theological and philosophical constructions. He is much bigger than my own culture, mother language and nation. He is infinitely much bigger than what we call "my religion." He is God. He is the Creator. He is not confined to any human system. As I see the vast blue ocean, the beautiful and immense green forests everywhere; as I am aware of the existence of millions and millions of stars and galaxies, thousands and thousands of mountains, valleys, rivers and waterfalls, I conclude that any individual will at least be agnostic. Yes, he or she would at least become agnostic due to those latent and constant external signs that work as an extrinsic voice of God. It seems that all people everywhere will at least say, "I do not know who and where God is, but God is there somewhere because

His presence and intelligence are undeniable when we consider Creation and the work of His hands."

Today science talks about absolute singularity. Some individuals affirm that there was intelligence, an absolute singularity, behind the Big Bang phenomenon. Let's say I find a watch on the ground. I would ask, "How was this watch made?" Some people might say the minute hand came from a piece of wood that went through several transformations due to external factors over a period of millions of years. After that, the hour hand was made due to strong winds and intense rains over millions of years, joining the minute hand somehow. The body of the watch came from a deep part of the ocean that dried after millions of years, joining the hour and minute hand, making this final product in a natural way. This could be an answer. Laws of nature would support it.

A different perspective might be: I found a watch. It says, "made in China" on it. I do not know who made it, but I know there was intelligence behind it. It is as simple as that. I see there is intelligence due to its shape, its dynamics, its synchronization and the way each piece is made with perfection. I do not know who made it, but I definitely suspect there is intelligence behind this creation. You may come across a mountain that seems to have the shapes of animal or human faces caused by thousands and thousands of years of external environment influences, concluding that the mountain was shaped by diverse and multiple natural reasons. But, if you find out you are looking at the Mount Rushmore National Memorial in the Black Hills of Keystone, South Dakota, United States, with the faces of George Washington, Thomas Jefferson, Theodore Roosevelt and Abraham Lincoln, it is clear that there is an undeniable intelligence behind it. Someone made those faces and shaped them in the mountain. After listening to some of my reflections, Pastor Gabriel, my Brazilian-Japanese friend, told me:
Fábio, a few years ago, I met a Native Brazilian (indigenous) from one of our tribes at a mission conference in Brazil.

Really?! What did he tell you?

He told me somehow he was aware of the fact there were "two Gods." One was a good God and had a son. The other one was not good, he was evil. This native man knew when he made "right" decisions, he pleased the good God. Very nice. And there was no missionary or church present in his tribe when he came to this conclusion? Not at all! When missionaries eventually got to his tribe, they told him about a loving and forgiving God who had a Son and sent him to die for our sins. He was not surprised because he already knew it!

Don Richardson, author of *Eternity in their Hearts*, gave several examples like this. This experience and Richardson's writings support what the apostle Paul says in Romans 2, "For it is not those who hear the law who are righteous in God's sight, but it is those who obey the law who will be declared righteous. (Indeed, when Gentiles, who do not have the law, do by nature things required by the law, they are a law for themselves, even though they do not have the law. They show that the requirements of the law are written on their hearts, their consciences also bearing witness, and their thoughts sometimes accusing them and at other times even defending them.) This will take place on the day when God judges people's secrets through Jesus Christ," (Romans 2:13-16).

Extrinsic and Intrinsic Voice of God

If nature is the extrinsic voice of God to all of humankind and civilization, from the first human being to the last one, then the second pillar, the conscience, is the intrinsic voice of God to all of humanity. Together, they, nature and our conscience, are witnesses of God. Millions of human beings undoubtedly have reached this point, face to face with God, experiencing His unconditional love and amazing grace because "His voice goes out through all the earth, and His words to the end of the world" (Psalm 19:4). I am aware of the fact that nature and our conscience do not tell me who God is, but both give me signs of God's goodness. For example, our conscience accuses or defends us, telling us what is good or bad, what we should or should not do. The older we get, the more we are influenced by our own culture, religious experience, childhood upbringing and other external factors that can cause us to drift gradually, losing our sensitivity to discern good and evil.

One could say when we decide to participate in "holy" wars and crusades on behalf of god, our intrinsic sense of good and evil is gone. But, I still believe, in spite of losing our sensitivity to good and evil, somehow, our conscience still has the possibility to be the intrinsic voice of God and a potential lamp into our heart. After all, Hebrews 1:1 tells us, "God spoke to our ancestors through the prophets many times and in various ways." Various ways might include historical events, personal experiences, dreams, visions, the beautiful and unspeakable Creation, our conscience as a lamp into my heart and an intuitive understanding of God's eternal love, and on and on. Therefore, people in all eras and everywhere have received at some point, somehow, a glimpse of His goodness, confirming that humankind is truly without excuse.

God Reveals God - Missio Dei

What have we learned so far? What does this point of view and perspective have to do with my missiological approach? What does this perception change in me and my worldview? Missio Dei is an understanding that God is able and free to reveal Godself to any culture or group of people at any moment in history to any civilization or whomever He decides to reveal Himself through any way because He is God, independent of you, me or any religious organization. Period. We could finish our debates and theological discussions here. Missio Dei is God's mission among civilizations, cultures, and peoples in all eras. At the same time, I know I am God's co-worker in His mission. I have a mission to proclaim the good news, I am a bridge between cultures, I am God's facilitator, I am part of His mission, however, I am not obligated or forced to become a pastor, evangelist, missionary announcing God's name everywhere. If I do not speak, this doesn't mean God will never show up. If I do speak and proclaim He is God, it doesn't mean I'll have a better place in heaven or that my heavenly home will be like those multi-million dollar homes I've seen in Miami - not at all! Rather, I assume my mission role in life, I embrace my missiological call, I say, "yes, here I am," because of the privilege, the love, the joy of carrying the message of Jesus Christ wherever I go. In short, it is absolutely my pleasure to transmit God's love with freedom by loving my neighbor and being an agent of reconciliation. Before we go ahead, let's remind ourselves that neither nature nor our conscience will be able to tell us exactly who God is, but they will work as fingerprints of His eternal and sublime love.

Chapter 11

The Scriptures and Jesus, the Son of God

"The Son of God became a man [sic] to enable men to become sons [sic] of God."
C. S. Lewis

For Bible Worshippers (be sure to read to the end)

The Scriptures bring me to the next level of perception. The Scriptures allow me to comprehend lucidly who God is, His image and dimension of His care and unconditional love for His creatures. The Scriptures testify about Jesus, the Son of God. In fact, all Scriptures take me to Jesus. Multiple authors, most of whom were not contemporaries, over a period of almost 1,500 years, produced what we have in our hands today known as the Bible. The apostle Peter says, "For prophecy never had its origin in the human will, but prophets, though human, spoke from God as they were carried along by the Holy Spirit" (2 Peter 1:21). The Scriptures are the testimony of Jesus. They show the fulfillment of God's progressive and gradual revelation through generations of civilizations throughout human history. The Scriptures point to the culmination of God's promise, Jesus Christ, the Eternal Christ of God, the Son of God. As those two men walked on the road to Emmaus and talked about the last happenings in Jerusalem, "He said to them, 'How foolish you are, and how slow to believe all that the prophets have spoken! Did not the Messiah have to suffer these things and then enter His glory?' And beginning with Moses and all the Prophets, he explained to them what was said in all the Scriptures concerning himself" (Luke 24:25-27).

Moses, all the Prophets, the Psalms - all the Scriptures - have spoken about Jesus. Jesus is the fulfillment of the prophecies, however, the religious groups 2,000 years ago were not able to see God's promise fulfilled before their very own eyes in Jesus. Jesus said to the Jewish leaders, "You study the Scriptures diligently because you think that in them you have eternal life. These are the very Scriptures that testify about me" (John 5:39). The Scriptures are the third pillar of God's voice to you and me. It is our privilege to have the Scriptures available, to read the prophecies and discern how everything in the past was just a foreshadowing of what would be the convergence of Jesus and God's plan of revelation and salvation. Peter's speech after Pentecost in Acts 2 and Stephen's speech to the Sanhedrin in Acts 7 are extensive attempts to bring Jewish historical events and the prophecies of the Old Testament to light, showing evidence that Jesus was the fulfillment of the One they were expecting, waiting for, asking for, in other words, the Messiah, the Christ. The apostle Paul said to the Galatians, "So the law was our guardian until Christ came that we might be justified by faith. Now that this faith has come, we are no longer under a guardian" (Galatians 3:24-25).

The law could be compared to a babysitter who takes care of us until we become adults, gain maturity and become aware of what we should and should not do. The Scriptures have been given to us progressively. God's revelation has been gradually given to us as we read how the Son of God became flesh in history. Luke, in his Gospel, after reading the prophet Isaiah in the synagogue, registered that Jesus said: "Today this scripture is fulfilled in your hearing" (Luke 4:21).

"All Scripture is God-breathed and is useful for teaching, rebuking, correcting and training in righteousness" (2 Timothy 3:16). Yes, I do agree that all Scriptures are God-breathed. The order in which most of us read them begins in Genesis with a description of a couple, then moves forward to two types of societies, agricultural and pastoral, continuing on to the development of cities, swords and battles. In spite of everything, we are still able to see how God's mercy, love, forgiveness and compassion prevail in a very primitive society, archaic mentality and era. What we observe is a historical road from legislation (what the Israelites could and could not do), a period of prophets and judges, to a theocratic regime, a monarchy system, and in and through it all, we observe how, somehow, somewhere, God's unspeakable revelation is used as a pedagogical instrument to demonstrate His love to humankind.

In fact, what fascinates me is to find out God's presence, instruction, care and unconditional love in each past generation even though their understanding and discernment could have been extremely relative and primitive. I am perplexed when I read "In the past God spoke to our ancestors through the prophets at many times and in various ways, but in these last days he has spoken to us by his Son, whom he appointed heir of all things, and through whom also he made the universe" (Hebrews 1:1-2). What does this journey have to do with our missiological awareness? What do these concepts have to do with the way we see life and all cultures in all eras in human history? How could these principles affect our spiritual journey today?

Please, do not forget our reflection cannot be only from a Western point of view. The world is not the United States of America. History did not start yesterday or even a few years ago. If we have countless differences among our cultures in the 21st Century, can you imagine how many different cultures, tribes, unique civilizations we have had in history? Many of them no longer exist today. In the past, millions of people may have perceived God through nature, through their internal voice as a glimpse of light, through the Scriptures, through exhortation by prophets or simply a face-to-face encounter with God in ways we cannot imagine. What we do know is that, at a certain point in history, "The Word became flesh and made his dwelling among us. We have seen his glory, the glory of the one and only Son, who came from the Father, full of grace and truth" (John 1:14).

God is Free Because God is God

In the past, God freely chose ways to reveal Himself to humans. He didn't ask permission from anyone as to how, where, when and to whom He should show up. For example, in John 3:14 we read, "just as Moses lifted up the snake in the wilderness, so the Son of Man must be lifted up." The snake was a representation and symbol of what would happen with Jesus. Jesus was also represented by the Ark of the Covenant. Jesus was the true manna - He said, "I am the living bread that came down from heaven. Whoever eats this bread will live forever. This bread is my flesh, which I will give for the life of the world" (John 6:51). Jesus is the true "Easter" or "Passover." Jesus is the Tabernacle. And more than that, after Jesus' resurrection, we realized the Eternal Christ's presence was actively present in the past. If Paul did not write the letter to the Corinthians, we would have never known Jesus was there. That Rock was Christ. "For I do not want you to be ignorant of the fact, brothers and sisters, that our ancestors were all under the cloud and that they all passed through the sea. They were all baptized into Moses in the cloud and in the sea. They all ate the same spiritual food and drank the same spiritual drink; for they drank from the spiritual rock that accompanied them, and that rock was Christ" (1 Corinthians 10:1-4). The Scriptures are God's words. The Scriptures contain God's words. The Scriptures are the most accurate material you and I could possibly have in our hands to see God's revelation and testimony, but it is not the only "word" of God. As we see, God spoke to our ancestors many times in various ways, therefore the Scriptures testify to and glorify Jesus. The Scriptures are the conductor to Jesus. But, Jesus is the Word of God. The Scriptures are absolutely inspired by God, but they are not divine. Jesus is Divine. Jesus is God. The Eternal Christ is God, therefore, the Bible is a book. The Scriptures are the text, and Jesus is the Word of God.

Sola scriptura (by Scripture alone) was one of the principles of the reformers in the 16th Century. The written word was absolutely crucial to Luther. Yet, even more important than the written word was the Living Word, Jesus Christ. Luther said, "The Bible was the crib wherein Christ leith."[54] The Scriptures without the living Christ is only ink on a page. The Bible has become "the mother of all heresies" in history. The Bible in the hands of someone without correct understanding of who Jesus is and his hermeneutic of love could be compared to a knife in the hands of a drunkard. You may find people who use the Bible as a good luck charm. If someone is having a heart attack, he might put the Bible against his chest and believe he will die closer to God. If someone is experiencing insomnia or a spiritual, emotional or psychological torment, she may put the Bible under her pillow to make the "ghosts" disappear. Some use the Bible as a type of horoscope. I call this phenomenon "Bibleroscopy." Have you heard of someone opening the Bible at random to find out what God has to say to him on that specific day and in that particular circumstance? There is a risk, it's like the lottery. They may open it and read, "Judas went away and hanged himself" (Matthew 27:5). Then they will say, "No this is not a good text, let me try again." Then, they find a new text and see, "Go and do likewise" (Luke 10:37). No way, God, please speak to me! One more time, "What you are about to do, do quickly" (John 13:27). These three texts in a row would be considered a devastating combination for a person who is not in an emotionally healthy space, the possible end to her life. The Bible is absolutely not meant to be used in this way.

Of course, the Bible contains differences when we compare the same genealogies in different books. You may find different counts of dead soldiers in different books even though they all talk about the same battles. You may find Jesus healing a blind man in one of the Gospels and two blind men in a different Gospel. But, the Bible has never claimed to be a scientific book. It is not an archeological book even though no archeological dig that takes place in Israel happens without the help of the Bible or *The Antiquities*[55] by Flavius

---

[54] *20th Century Theology: God & the World in a Transitional Age* by Stanley J. Grenz, Roger E. Olson, Page 82.

[55] The Antiquities of the Jews: Completed and Unabridged by Flavius Josephus, Copyright 2012, Renaissance Classics.

Josephus, the Roman-Jewish scholar and historian of the 1st Century.

More important than a precise genealogy tree is to understand that Jesus came from David's lineage and was the fulfillment of God's countless promises since Adam. More important than proving if there was one or two blind men in the context was the fact that Jesus healed individuals who came his way. David Nyvall, the first president of North Park Seminary said, "Go to the Bible with an eye only for error and contradiction, grammatical anomalies, historical errors, mistaken data and numbers, and the Bible is big enough for a scholarship only for those things. But go to it with an eye for the life that billows forth in mighty waves in the water course, burst here and there, and you will be rewarded infinitely more. The Bible is a world that should be studied with a telescope rather than a microscope. What a loss it would be to study the stars or the northern lights with a magnifying glass."[56]

Millions of people have found Jesus without the Scriptures. Not just in our generation, but throughout time, millions have not heard or seen one verse of the Scriptures. Can you imagine how many people right now might be receiving a vision, dream or divine insight without ever having access to the Bible? And for those who do have access, how many people in how many countries today cannot even open the Scriptures to read or study them because it's against the law? How many cultures and political regimes punish people who speak the Scriptures aloud? And now what about those who have access and can read it legally, but do not have the ability to read? If we have illiteracy still today, just imagine the rates of illiteracy hundreds of years ago.

As mentioned before, the Catholic Church that represented the voice of Christianity beginning in the 4th Century imprisoned the Scriptures until the 16th Century when Luther translated them and made them accessible to anyone in German. Thankfully, we have the ability to read the Scriptures in our language since a German man named Johannes Gutenberg developed the printing press around the year 1440. And what about before that? Did God really not speak to

---

[56] *Living Faith* by the Faculty of North Park Theological Seminary, page 26.

anyone without the Scriptures? Was God confined in a book? Of course not! Books are a recent invention. Before the invention of the book, texts were kept on parchments or enormous scrolls or documents in vases like those manuscripts found in the Qumran Caves near the Dead Sea. Today we have access to the Scriptures through our iPhones and iPads. Sometimes we forget it has not always been that way. But God is not confined in a book! Was God able to speak to those cultures and civilizations before access, before legality, before literacy? The answer is yes, yes and yes! He was able. He is free. He is God.

As I travel and talk to Western Christians, it seems that most of them think the entire world is like the United States or Latin America, filled with thousands of churches, evangelical TV and radio programs, Gospel concerts and Christian holidays to celebrate with their families each year. Unfortunately, they may know a few theories, but cannot even imagine how it is forbidden to convert someone to a different religion in some countries where Islam is the law. They can't imagine what it's like to live in a place like Japan where Christianity is represented by less than 1% of the population. The world was not born the day we were born. It hasn't always been like it is now, a technological and fast world in which to move, travel, send and receive pictures, movies and have immediate access to information. There is an accumulation of thousands of years behind us, countless civilizations, millions who lived before us.

A few years ago, I read the biography of Sadhu Sudar Singh. The book is called *O Apóstolo dos Pés Sangrentos,*[57] meaning the Apostle with Bleeding Feet, based on his nickname. Sadhu Sudar Singh was an Indian missionary born in India in 1889 who probably died in the Himalayas in 1929. He asked for the manifestation of the True God and said if he did not appear before him, he would kill himself. So, a certain night, he received a vision of Jesus who opened his heart and eyes to the truth. Although many Western Christians tried to change his Indian dress, he kept wearing a turban and the yellow robe of a Hindu sadhu, because he knew Jesus' message could not be effective in India unless it was given in an

---

[57] *O Apóstolo dos pés Sangrentos* by Boanerges Ribeiro, CPAD.

Indian way.[58]

How many people are having experiences like Sadhu Sudar Singh right now in some part of the world? How many tribes and peoples are having a glimpse of God's revelation right now in the isolated Pacific, unreachable Middle East and Southeast Asia? What about a mom who observes the beautiful and divine miracle of her pregnancy, but then faces the fact that she could lose her baby at any moment? She cries out and says, "If there is a God, please save my baby and I will devote my life to Him even though I do not know where and who He is." How many people have had near-death experiences and then come back as better fathers, better friends, better sons and daughters, better human beings by learning how to love, forgive, practice hospitality and be merciful because they have faced "the Light" and cannot even explain their glimpse of a divine experience? Someday we will be surprised to find ourselves facing many people who have met Jesus and did not know He was Jesus. And that Rock was Christ!

Many will come from everywhere and join the heavenly and divine feast, "I say to you that many will come from the east and the west, and will take their places at the feast with Abraham, Isaac and Jacob in the kingdom of heaven" (Matthew 8:11). We cannot box up God's ways trying to define how He communicates with humankind. We cannot limit God's ways and establish formulas to determine how God reveals Himself over time, throughout eras and civilizations. However, we can affirm that the Scriptures lead us to comprehend who Jesus was, what he came to do, and who God is by showing us the way to live through love and acts of justice and mercy.

Jesus is my hermeneutic key as I go through the Scriptures, observing the laws, prophecies, Psalms and Jewish ceremonies. He is present in the Old Testament, hidden in every archetype. Even though 2,000 years ago religious groups knew the Scriptures by

---

[58] I recommend reading his short biography in *The Apostle with Bleeding Feet*: Sadhu Sundar Singhon [Written for World Christianity taught by Dr. Guy Lytle, 5/8/04] on http://frjody.com/writings/the-apostle-with-bleeding-feet-sadhu-sundar-singh/

heart, they couldn't recognize the Messiah nor the fulfillment of what they had memorized. Those Scribes, Pharisees, exegetics of the law and hermeneutics of religion read the texts of the Scriptures over and over every week, every Sabbath at the temple or synagogue, but one could argue they didn't read God's Word. It sounds like a paradox or ambiguity, but though they knew the Scriptures, they were unable to discern God's Word, Jesus Christ, right in front of their eyes. If we read the Scriptures without Jesus, then the letter might kill us because only the Spirit gives life. "He has made us competent as ministers of a new covenant - not of the letter but of the Spirit; for the letter kills, but the Spirit gives life" (2 Corinthians 3:6). If we read the Scriptures without Jesus as our absolute centrality, they will only become pages of historical events. The Bible, "Biblos" in Greek, meaning "book", is a library of sixty-six books, containing texts and descriptions that point to the Word of God, Jesus Christ, the Eternal Christ of God. Today, God continues to speak by the Spirit through the Scriptures, which remain our main source for reflection and study. However, I become afraid when I see people almost worshipping the Bible and giving it the same level of worship in their lives that Jesus is supposed to have. Jesus died on the cross, not the Bible. "God was in Christ reconciling the world to Himself, not imputing their trespasses to them, and has committed to us the word of reconciliation" (2 Corinthians 5:19, NKJV). The apostles never worshipped the Scriptures. They never even knew their writings would become what we know today as the Bible.

The incarnation of Jesus didn't happen in a book. God was not bound to ink and pages. God was incarnate, in flesh and blood. Jesus resurrected from the dead, not the Bible. He is the only One to be worshipped. In the Bible, we read about his life and teachings. Each one of the apostles knew that what they were writing was to encourage groups of believers and churches - it was the truth that came from Jesus' teachings. At the same time, they knew the only Word of God was Jesus, the Eternal Christ, the One who became human and lived among them. For example, Genesis 12 says God's word came to Abraham much before the existence of the Scriptures. The text tells us "Now the Lord had said to Abram: 'Get out of your country, from your family and from your father's house, to a land that I will show you. I will make you a great nation: I will bless you, and make your name great; and you shall be a blessing.'"

God's word came to the magi without the Scriptures, they were pagans. In Matthew 2:1-2 (NKJV), we read "wise men from the East came to Jerusalem, saying, 'Where is He who has been born King of the Jews? For we have seen His star in the east and have come to worship Him.'"

How many ways is God able to reveal Himself to a certain group of people, culture or individual? Does God select a few cultures and reject others? Has God chosen a certain side of the earth to bless, giving them access to the Scriptures while neglecting others? How can we understand God's freedom? How can we find balance regarding the centrality of the Scriptures in order to have access to God's promises, Jesus' life and teachings, and our privilege to have them available to be read freely in our mother tongue without hierarchical or clerical influence? How can we have the crucial understanding that Jesus IS the Living Word of God who becomes our filter and hermeneutic key whenever we read the Scriptures?

In short, we have seen the Living Word of God who is not confined in any book or group of doctrines or theological system. This Living Word is not confined as a dilemma between Calvinists and Armenians, He is not stuck in a certain religion. The Living Word of God is not limited to a certain culture or people, either. He is God. Against hypocrisy, false piety, religiosity as a mechanism, the prophet Malachi exhorts the Israelites saying, "'Who is there even among you who would shut the doors, so that you would not kindle fire on my altar in vain? I have no pleasure in you,' says the Lord of hosts, 'nor will I accept an offering from your hands. For from the rising of the sun, even to its going down, my name shall be great among the Gentiles; In EVERY PLACE incense shall be offered to my name, and a pure offering; for my name shall be great among THE NATIONS' says the Lord of hosts" (emphasis mine; Malachi 1:10-11, NKJV)

We frequently face polarizations in most of our theological tensions. If some individuals "worship" the Scriptures on one hand, others like Marcion of Sinope[59] who lived in Pontus (modern-day

---

[59] You can read a brief commentary on the article, "Marcion: Portrait of a Heretic by Robert Bradshaw" at https://earlychurch.org.uk/article_marcion.html

eastern Black Sea Region of Turkey) in the 2nd Century, denigrated and devalued the Old Scriptures by erroneously proposing two different gods, one in the Old Testament and another in the New Testament. The Church Fathers condemned his theology and ideas. Marcion wanted to keep only Paul's letters and the Gospel of Luke because Luke was a disciple of Paul. He did not consider the Old Testament to be a source that testified and confirmed Jesus as the Christ. The paradox was striking because it is exactly in Luke that we find Jesus himself saying that all the Scriptures pointed to Him. "Then He said to them, 'O foolish ones, and slow of heart to believe in all that the prophets have spoken! Ought not the Christ to have suffered these things and to enter into His glory?' And beginning at Moses and all the Prophets, He expounded to them in all the Scriptures the things concerning Himself" (Luke 24: 25-27).

Those of us from the West have all heard about Jesus. We learned that he was born in Bethlehem, walked in Jerusalem and Galilee and other parts of Palestine in the 1st Century. He manifested His goodness among us, died on the cross, was resurrected from the dead and then, the Eternal Christ revealed Himself to you and me, so today we follow Jesus Christ. In our case, or most of us, we received this historical information before any revelation. The apostle Paul says, "for in Christ all the fullness of the Deity lives in bodily form," (Colossians 2:9). Jesus is God. One of the moments when Jesus' identity became the clearest was when Philip said, "Lord, show us the Father and that will be enough for us. Jesus answered: 'Don't you know me, Philip, even after I have been among you such a long time? Anyone who has seen me has seen the Father. How can you say, 'Show us the Father'? Don't you believe that I am in the Father, and that the Father is in me? The words I say to you I do not speak on my own authority. Rather, it is the Father, living in me, who is doing his work. Believe me when I say that I am in the Father and the Father is in me; or at least believe on the evidence of the works themselves'" (John 14:8-11).

What fascinates me is to understand that usually people are condemned for what they do. However, Jesus was condemned and killed for what He said. This fact is evident when we read what John wrote regarding the religious groups and their intentions to catch and incriminate Jesus: "Again, his Jewish opponents picked up stones to stone him, but Jesus said to them, 'I have shown you many good works from the Father. For which of these do you stone me?' 'We are not stoning you for any good work,' they replied, 'but for blasphemy, because you, a mere man, claim to be God'" (John 10:31-33). The author of Hebrews declares, "The Son is the radiance of God's glory and the exact representation of his being, sustaining all things by his powerful word" (Hebrews 1:3). He is the exact representation of God.

Lunatic or Honest?

Although Jesus could be considered a lunatic, although he could have had an insane, megalomaniac and narcissistic personality, we would have to consider him to have a lucid insanity because no one has ever spoken like him. When the guards were sent to arrest him: "'No one ever spoke the way this man does,' the guards replied" (John 7:46). Philosophers, thinkers and intellectuals have tried to understand Jesus' personality, but not one psychological instrument or trained person has been able to detect his "craziness." This pushes us into a corner. Jesus' "lucid insanity," in short, leaves us with only one option. If he was not a liar or a lunatic, he must have been who he said he was: God. He doesn't offer an alternative. More than that, "The Son is the image of the invisible God, the firstborn over all creation. For in him all things were created: things in heaven and on earth, visible and invisible, whether thrones or powers or rulers or authorities; all things have been created through him and for him. He is before all things, and in him all things hold together" (Colossians 1:15-17). No one has ever seen God. No one. No angel. No human being. "No one has ever seen God, but the one and only Son, who is himself God and is in closest relationship with the Father, has made him known" (John 1:18). It is an indescribable and unspoken mystery. God Himself, verified in Jesus. God Himself, available in Jesus. Not to be studied, but to be experienced. Not to be analyzed, but to be proven in our hearts as a personal and tangible experience of love.

Jesus puts us face to face with God when we see Him. We are able to understand how God sees the poor, marginalized, pagans, the centurion and how God responds to religious groups, hypocrisy, fanaticism, radicalism, manipulation and other matters when we see

Jesus responding to each circumstance in life. I learn how the Father is when I read the parables of Jesus. I understand how God is a God of abundance, joy and "feast," a party God, how He rejoices as a father when, in the story of the Prodigal Son, his son comes back home. The parable of the Good Samaritan invites us to be like the one who helped the wounded man on the road in spite of the many cultural, political and religious differences. Jesus' parables also teach us how sincerity and honesty are ingredients needed for God to hear our prayers, such as in the parable of the Pharisee and the tax collector. As well as I may know what God is like in Jesus, I also learn how we may become more human. In Jesus, we have a glimpse of how to discern God. We learn that justice and equality are important matters. We learn that from the heart proceeds evil things, therefore, we should watch our heart and its deepest motivations. We learn that there are no secrets hidden before God's eyes. Also, it is through Jesus that we learn how to read the Scriptures. It is through Jesus that we learn how to talk to our Heavenly Father.

Once again, Jesus is the hermeneutic key through whom we respond to all aspects of life. We have seen how nature can perplex us as we observe God's Creation, but we may not go farther than that. Our conscience may yell at us, allowing us to discern good from evil, yet over time, our external context, backgrounds, family experience and culture might make us numb, causing us to lose this ability. Though Creation undoubtedly gives us glimpses of God, none of our experiences will put us in God's lap. So, what can we conclude about the Scriptures from these last pages? And Jesus - who is He after all? The Scriptures have been teaching us about God's mercy, love and purpose throughout history. They testify about and glorify Jesus, but it is only in Jesus that we can discern who God is. He is the image of the invisible God.

Chapter 12

Belief in Jesus does not require intellectual suicide

"Leap of faith – yes, but only after reflection."
Søren Kierkegaard.

What is Jesus Proposing?

Jesus offers a road to humankind untraveled by many people. But it is only in Jesus that you and I have a chance to palpate God. It is not a coincidence that Paul says, "For the message of the cross is foolishness to those who are perishing, but to us who are being saved it is the power of God" (1 Corinthians 1:18). Why was the message of the cross foolishness for the Jews? Why didn't this religious group recognize and receive Jesus as their Messiah? Why couldn't they understand Jesus? Obviously, the answers to these questions could be discussed for hours and hours. In short, the Jews were expecting someone to restore the kingdom of Israel. They expected someone to defeat the Roman Emperor who had dominated Palestine and many parts of the world. They couldn't see how these expectations and divine promises delivered by several prophets and God's provision to their salvation and restoration might be met in the person of Jesus.

Why was the same message of the cross foolishness for the Greeks? Would they be able to accept Jesus as God incarnate? Could the Greeks understand the message of a loving, eternal and absolute God who would die for such pitiful, finite and selfish human beings? The Greeks had a pantheon of gods. They could never imagine that God would go through the humiliation of being crucified on a cross. They could never imagine God nailed to a piece of wood between two murderers. They couldn't picture God being tortured by guards and accused by political-religious groups without reacting in a forceful way in order to avoid the penalty of death. Foolishness!

Why was the message of the cross foolishness for the Romans? A God who put on skin and lived among human beings and then died on a cross? A God who walked with murderers, prostitutes, publicans and people on the margins of society? What kind of powerful God is this? Is this even power? The Romans may have thought, "This isn't power! For us, power is to dominate, impose ideas and ideologies. Power is to conquer and reign, establishing rules to be obeyed. Is Jesus the Son of God? What does that even mean? If there is a small chance it can be truth, how can he be accused and defeated by human religious systems? What about the cross? How could he allow himself to be killed in the most miserable and shameful way?" Never! It is foolishness! As I learned from Thomas Carlyle, a Scottish philosopher, even if Jesus was not a historical person, the mind of his creator would be considered a brilliant and fascinating mind, almost divine.

In Mark 4, after Jesus rebuked the wind and the sea, "Peace, be still!" the wind stopped and there was a great calm. The disciples said to each other, "Who can this be, that even the wind and the sea obey Him?" In a different occasion in Luke 9, Jesus asked, "Who do the crowds say that I am?" and they said, "Some say John the Baptist, others say Elijah; and still others, that one of the old prophets of long ago has come back to life." Jesus said to them, "Who do you say that I am?" Peter answered and said, "God's Messiah" (Luke 9:18-20). Who was that man? This is the question. Who was Jesus? The one who walked in Galilee, ate with tax collectors and sinners, received those who were rejected by society and religious groups.

Who was Jesus?

Jesus may have been 5 feet 6 inches tall and spent time hanging out with those who were marginalized and had no voice. The Jewish scholar and historian named Josephus said that Jesus was like one of the Nazarenes. He dressed like one of them. He could even be confused as one until he started speaking and teaching, because that's when people saw no one taught like him. No one said what Jesus said. Jesus was fully man and fully God. Jesus was one hundred percent man and one hundred percent God. Jesus was God because he let himself be adored. In Matthew 8, we read about a leper who came and worshiped Him. No one was supposed to receive worship. No one. No angel nor human was supposed to be adored - only God. He also forgave sins. No one could forgive sins except God. Jesus was also a man. He ran, he cried, he sweated, he ate, drank and lived life while splitting history into two parts - before and after Him. He was spirit clothed in flesh and blood. He was a synthesis of human and divine, both man and God.

In the past, there were rumors and attempts to deny the validity of the historical Jesus. Today, it is almost considered impossible to try to deny his existence. However, I should admit that although one tries to put all the historical and logical pieces of Jesus and his life together, there will always be a moment when one is invited to take a leap of faith. I know my mind and intellect are able to get to a certain point following logical reflection, but after a while, it becomes foolish to try to explain what is not explainable. I have just enough intelligence to understand that I cannot reach God through my human philosophical and logical constructions. Many people think you have to commit intellectual suicide to believe in God. It is a lie. We know that no relative being can reach out to the one who is Absolute. We understand that it is impossible, scientifically speaking, to prove the existence or nonexistence of the divine, and if we could do it, he would no longer be divine. Since he is Spirit, our experience with the Divine must be in the geography of our hearts. For me, experiencing God is the most objective-personal-subjective experience that any human can have.

Blaise Pascal was a French mathematician, physicist, inventor, writer and philosopher. He said, "The heart has its reasons which reason knows nothing of."[60] We barely have answers regarding our complex body system, often kidnapped by diseases that are never healed. We live in an era where more and more people struggle with mental and psychosomatic disorders, we don't understand the power of our emotions and mind, we do not know how to handle complicated local and global social issues, and we definitely feel powerless in the face of our political and economical chaos. Personally, I do not understand why my stomach doesn't react badly when I eat ham, but cannot process other pork products. Or why I can eat yogurt and cheese, but not milk without feeling sick to my stomach. We may not understand why we lose our temper easily. Do you understand your body and emotions well? Can you explain how your hormones work? Scientific theories change constantly. We cannot absolutely define our galaxies and universe in great detail. We are permanently looking for answers and updating our concepts.

Raise Your Hand if You Understand God's Mind

How can we try to understand God and act as if we can read His mind? How can we, little worms, begin to study the One who is Absolute? How can we pretend to put God on a surgical table and dissect him to figure out His ways? How can we imprison God in a religious system? How can we possibly think that the God of the universe could fit into our philosophical thoughts? You may ask me, "But what is faith? What does it mean? How can I conclude that faith is not intellectual suicide, yet at the same time, I can't provide anything to prove God exists in a logical way? It sounds like a contradiction. It sounds like a labyrinth with no exit." First of all, I usually describe the difference between belief and faith. I may have grown up in a Christian home, have learned how to pray, I may open my Bible, know how to play guitar or even be an eloquent preacher. But, this doesn't mean I have a personal relationship with Jesus as

---

[60] Cited on https://www.brainyquote.com/quotes/quotes/b/blaisepasc132990.html

my friend and Lord. It may be more like a religious, superficial experience I learned from my local church culture, denominational culture or Christian belief. I may have perfected the art of being like everyone else who comes from the same environment. However, faith is much deeper. Faith is a personal experience with God. It is the deepest and most honest thing I may have in my heart. It is not a performance. Faith makes me say radical things like Job, "Naked I came from my mother's womb and naked I will depart. The Lord gave and the Lord has taken away; may the name of the Lord be praised" (Job 1:21).

Some people may get impressed with someone who is a missionary or pastor, speaking in the pulpit, pretending he or she is on stage in a theater. It might be easy for this person to deceive his or her parents. It is so easy to deceive a boss, colleagues and even close friends. How about the spouse and children? It is not complicated to deceive them. It is even easy to deceive ourselves. But God cannot be deceived. God is always searching for much more than my appearance, my performance, the way things appear from the outside. He looks at my heart. He is looking for me to show my true self, my true personality, knowing my best and worst parts. He is looking for who you and I truly and genuinely are because God is looking for individuals who worship him in spirit and in truth.

Second, faith has nothing to do with logic even though I use logical arguments to write and talk about God. Faith has nothing to do with rationalism even though I use rational thoughts to express and share my faith experiences. Faith has nothing to do with logic and rationalism because I cannot construct any human system that is able to talk about God in a way that will result in proving his very existence. Following this thinking, I cannot be proud of our theology, either. It is arrogance and prepotency to think we are able to prove and study God through our systematic theology. The word, "theology" comes from the Greek words, "theos" meaning God and "logia" meaning word, discount, account and reasoning. It is basically the logical study of God. The study of animals is called zoology, the study of living organisms is called biology. But the study of God? Who can pretend to study the Divine? Who can pretend to study the infinite while being finite? In these writings, I'm using historical events, cultural contexts, the credibility of written texts of the gospels and apostles' letters in the New Testament, studying the history of religions, as well as other geographical, social, economic and political components of our civilization to construct a logical and rational foundation as far as I can as a limited human being.

There is one more component in my faith. It is a mystic experience even though it is outside of mysticism. What does that mean? What is the difference between having a mystic experience and mysticism? Well, any type of "ism" is a type of systematization, but faith is a mystic experience because it is personal, subjective, transcendental and spiritual. It is not mysticism because it has nothing to do with magic tricks, magic formulas, Aladdin's lamp, or any "abracadabra" that will produce a successful career, Hollywood marriage or life in Wonderland as a woman named Alice. When the author of Hebrews defines faith, his heart is full of logical thoughts and arguments, he evokes historical facts and events from his past, tangible and explainable experiences, but he also projects his future in a subjective, unexplainable and intangible hope because he is aware of the fact that faith is a logical-mystic path, but not magical. He beautifully says, "Now faith is confidence in what we hope for and assurance about what we do not see," (Hebrews 11:1).

One thing about Jesus that I find fascinating is seen when Jesus is talking to the Samaritan woman at the well: "Woman," Jesus replied, "believe me, a time is coming when you will worship the Father neither on this mountain nor in Jerusalem. You Samaritans worship what you do not know; we worship what we do know, for salvation is from the Jews. Yet a time is coming and has now come when the true worshipers will worship the Father in the Spirit and in truth, for they are the kind of worshipers the Father seeks. God is spirit, and his worshipers must worship in the Spirit and in truth" (John 4:21-24).

Jesus Christ is the Historical Eternal Christ of God

God allows Himself to be found when His worshipers seek Him in spirit and in truth. It's as simple as that. Truth, sincerity without masks, transparency without hypocrisy, an attitude of complete surrender without bargaining. God "cannot resist" anyone with these characteristics who tries to get close to Him. Jesus is the historical manifestation of the Eternal Christ of God. Before Jesus Christ existed, the Eternal Christ of God was. The Eternal Christ is timeless. Jesus Christ established a historical time for the Eternal Christ of God: "In the beginning the Word already existed. The Word was with God, and the Word was God" (John 1:1). Therefore, we can understand the apostle John when he writes, "The Lamb of God was slain before the foundation of the world" (Revelation 13:8). The historical cross may have been placed in the ground 2,000 years ago in Jerusalem in that space and during that time, however, the eternal cross was raised before the foundation of the world. It is no coincidence that later, Peter says, "He was chosen before the creation of the world, but was revealed in these last times for your sake" (1 Peter 1:20). Thousands of years before Jesus was born, the Eternal Christ was already there. I like to see how God is outside space and time. I like to see how God is above and beyond our presumptions and attempts to try to study, understand, and define Him.

"But you, Bethlehem Ephrathah, though you are small among the clans of Judah, out of you will come for me one who will be ruler over Israel whose origins are from of old, from ancient times" (Micah 5:2). From ancient times, Jesus Christ is the Word. Jesus Christ is the Eternal Christ. Jesus Christ is the Lamb of God. Jesus Christ was also the Angel of the Lord in the past. While growing up, I heard the definition of theophany many times. Coming from Ancient Greek, "Θεοφάνια" (theophania) means "the appearance of a god." We may all know that the ANGEL OF THE LORD (in capital letters) was the manifestation of Christ in the Old Testament. He was there. The Angel of the Lord is the Eternal Christ of God, which in Jesus Christ becomes the historical version.[61]

---

[61] In the Old Testament, the Angel of the Lord appeared several times. He appeared to Hagar (Gen 16:7-13), to Abraham and Isaac (Gen 22:9-18), in the burning bush (Exo 3:2-10), brought God's people out of Egypt (Num 20:16), opposed Balaam (Num 22:22-35), brought God's people to the Promised Land (Judges 2:1-4), cursed those who failed to help Israel (Judges 5:23), raised up Gideon (Judges 6:11-24), raised up Samson (Judges 13:13-22), brought judgment on Israel (2 Sam 24:15-17; 1 Chronicles 21:12-27), ministered to Elijah (1 Kings

How does this awareness of the Eternal Christ help me in my missiological journey? How does this understanding alter my view of God? How can we reconcile God's freedom to act as God wishes at any time, for any civilization, culture or people group in any era, with my personal theological convictions? God's freedom is not just a New Testament reality when we read, "The wind blows wherever it pleases. You hear its sound, but you cannot tell where it comes from or where it is going. So it is with everyone born of the Spirit." (John 3:8). God's freedom is present and has been present in all periods of history.

Who preached to Melchizedek, king of Salem and priest of the God Most High? (Genesis 14:18). Who brought a divine dream to the insane Nebuchadnezzar to cause him to raise his eyes toward heaven, praise the Most High, honor and glorify Him and declare His dominion as eternal? (Daniel 4). Approximately 1,400 years before Jesus Christ, who preached in Bochim, the place of weeping to the Israelites (Judges 2)? The Angel of the Lord!

Why did Jesus say to the religious people: "Your father Abraham rejoiced at the thought of seeing my day; he saw it and was glad" (John 8:56)? Because Jesus was there with Abraham in Genesis 18. The Eternal Christ of God, Jesus, was at the ford of the Jabbok in Genesis 32:22-31. He fought with Jacob; it was the Eternal Christ of God, the Angel of the Lord. Jesus is the fourth pillar by which we recognize God's voice and discern God's extraordinary love for humankind. At this point, you may be thinking, "Well, what can we learn from all of this?" We keep building a cathedral of thoughts, spiraling up and up, but my hope is that it will push you to take a quantum leap in order to understand how God is much bigger than our theories, theological thoughts, shallow philosophical understandings and limited ideas regarding God's Mission and evangelism in the world.

You may ask me, "Fábio, I know this happened in the past, but do you believe Jesus, the Eternal Christ, continues to show up today?" My response: Who preached to Saul on the road of Damascus? Who

19:1-7, 2 Kings 1:3, 15), killed 185,000 troops in one night, (2 Kings 19:35) and also opposed the accusations of Satan (Zechariah 3:1-10).

said, "Saul, Saul, why do you persecute me?" Was it one of Jesus' apostles? The answer is negative. When Saul asked, "Who are you, Lord?" the reply came, "I am Jesus, whom you are persecuting," (Acts 9:5). After his ascension, Jesus appeared to Saul. We have heard about several experiences among Muslims where people have had dreams about Jesus or Isa (the Arabic name for Jesus used by Muslims). Yes, the Eternal Christ of God continues to reveal himself because he is Eternal. These happenings, dreams and visions are not new; they are constantly mentioned in the Old and New Testaments. For example, look at the episode between Abraham and King Abimelech of Gerar who took Sarah as his wife because Abraham told him that Sarah was his sister. God came to Abimelech at night in a dream and said, "You are about to die because of the woman you have taken; for she is a married woman" (Genesis 20:2-3). As mentioned before, God's word preceded the written Scriptures and came to Abraham before he would have the possibility to hold them in his hands and read them. The divine revelation may precede the historical information any time in any civilization or for any culture or human being.

I enjoy reading the text of Cornelius, a centurion who was part of the Italian Regiment in Caesarea. He was a pagan, a Roman. But he was a devout man who, along with his entire household, feared God. He served others and lived in truth, honesty and simplicity. The text goes on to say that he gave generously and prayed continuously to God. How could a pagan, Roman centurion pray to God? How could God hear his prayer?

One afternoon around three o'clock, Acts 10 says he had a vision in which he clearly saw an angel of God come in and say to him, "Cornelius." He stared at him in terror and said, "What is it, Lord?" The Lord answered, "Your prayers and your gifts to the poor have come up as a memorial offering before God" (Acts 10:4). At the time Cornelius had this vision he had not heard about Jesus the Messiah, the historical Christ of God. However, if we keep reading, we see Peter was called to talk to Cornelius and let him know that God anointed Jesus of Nazareth with the Holy Spirit to die and be raised again on the third day. Peter was resistant to talk to Cornelius due to the fact that he was a Gentile, but three men from Cornelius' house came looking for him. It shows once again that God is free to reveal Himself to whomever He wants to. The divine revelation can precede historical information.

I was still a teenager when I read through the whole Bible. I read Jesus' narratives and the New Testament several times between ages twelve to sixteen. My mom took care of my grandmother who had metastasis. She also took care of my grandfather who had suffered a serious stroke. In addition, she took care of my sister and me, helped my father in the accounting office and kept a clean house - laundry, dishes, dusting, etc. The fact is I knew several biblical texts by heart, I knew the content of Paul's letters and their cultural contexts very well, but my mom didn't have time to read the Bible and for years, wasn't able to attend our local church. And yet, I have never seen anyone else live out Jesus' teachings and commandments in such an incarnational way. Many times growing up I thought to myself, "How does my mom know exactly what Jesus is asking us to do if she barely reads the Bible? How can she understand what I have been studying and learning in church if she's never in Sunday School?" As I observed her way of responding to life's challenges, I asked her, "Did you know what you are doing is exactly what Jesus says to do in Matthew chapter…? Did you know what you are saying is exactly what Jesus asked us to do in Luke chapter…?" I am not surprised now to look back on my experience with my mom and understand how God can reveal His will to any human being. I'm no longer surprised when I meet countless people around the world who barely know anything of the historical Christ, but have the Gospel in their hearts. The revelation may precede the historical information of Jesus, therefore, the Eternal Christ is actively showing His will and creating beautiful people all around the world.

There is not even one who has not been exposed to the Light that enlightens everyone

Well, let us consider how from the 4th Century to the 16th Century only popes, bishops and the clerical clan had access to the Scriptures because they claimed to be the only authorized representatives of God on earth. How many people died in Europe without knowing the historical Jesus as told by the Gospel narratives? How many native people in the Americas (South, Central, North) died without having a personal experience with missionaries or Westerners? How about in

Asia (Southeast, Middle East, countless islands) hundreds and hundreds of years ago? How many people passed away without ever knowing the existence of the historical Jesus? How many people today still connect Jesus to Christianity as a religious phenomenon or see it as a Western religion without knowing the true Jesus from the Gospels? What was the final destination for the millions of people who were never part of a Christian church or local denomination? I do not have an answer for most of these questions because I am not the Secretary of the Holy Trinity, but one thing I am sure, Jesus was active during those dark centuries in Europe. Jesus has been blowing his Spirit through the Middle East, Asia and Southeast Asia for hundreds of years in ways that you and I cannot even imagine. Millions have come face to face with Jesus without ever knowing that he was the Eternal Christ of God.

I will not hesitate to affirm that millions of people throughout time have had a glimpse of a divine revelation of God without ever receiving the historical information of Jesus. I am a relative and finite being, I live in space and time, but God is eternal and free to blow His Spirit wherever He wants. He is described as, "the true light that gives light to everyone was coming into the world" (John 1:9). God gives and gave light not just to our contemporaries, but to every single person in any era or civilization. Manifestations of God are perhaps reaching out to people much more than we can possibly imagine. We announce the historical Christ with our own limited comprehension today, but God is, right now, working at an unimaginable scale compared to all human tools and efforts to reveal God to others. He continues to bring light to countless places and people around the globe. Places where there are no missionaries or churches. In short, just as God did with Saul on the Damascus road and with the Roman centurion, Cornelius, the Eternal Christ is manifesting Himself as the Angel of God. He is in the refugee camps in Europe. He is speaking to some of the ISIS integrants through a vision or dream to convert them from their evil attitudes to a new heart with justice and peace. He is showing up in Islamic locations and to unreachable tribes. Every time there is a sincere crying out, an honest human being seeking God in spirit and truth, Jesus is there. Jesus will reveal Himself even when people don't have access to the Scriptures or to any church or to any missionary. Jesus is there, the Eternal Christ of God.

So, what is my role? How can I be part of this Missio Dei? It is simple. I announce the historical Jesus. I am an ambassador of the Good News. I offer any person the chance to know Jesus through the Gospels. I encourage them to have a better understanding of Jesus through the Scriptures. This is my role, however, I can trust that Jesus is the Light who will bring light to all people with or without my help. He does not depend on me to be the light of the world for He is the Light of the world. I join His mission with joy and proclaim to all the message that, "God was in Christ, reconciling the world to himself, no longer counting people's sins against them" (2 Corinthians 5:19). I had the privilege of receiving historical information before a divine revelation. Today, Christ grows in me. Today, I pursue the mind of Christ, meaning, I learn to see life through His eyes and teachings. Today, I know God's mission is bigger than any denomination, set of doctrines, biblical certificates or credentials. I am aware that God's mission is infinitely more efficient than my futile attempts at announcing the historical Jesus. Today, evangelism is my life, prayer is my life and life is my prayer. My mission and life are intrinsically integrated. I offer myself to be a living sacrifice and spread Jesus' message through my attitude and words. With that, everything changes. My concepts change, my terminologies change. My questions and answers change. There is no place left for questions such as, "Who is a Christian? Who is not? Who is saved? Who is lost? Who is going to heaven? Who is not?"

The concept of Church changes. Church is the assembly of saints, the gathering of the saints who have met the Eternal Christ face to face even if they have not known the historical Jesus. And Church is the gathering of those who met the Eternal Christ through the historical Jesus. Church is an impossible mission to describe because our natural eyes are not able to discern the dimension, exact number or amplitude of those who are servants of the Almighty God and who have been instruments making this world a better place to live despite its discrepancies, injustices, ambiguities and paradoxes.

Jesus said in the parable of the weeds and wheat: "Let both grow together until the harvest. At that time I will tell the harvesters: First collect the weeds and tie them in bundles to be burned; then gather the wheat and bring it into my barn" (Matthew 13:29). How can our small thoughts be impacted by what has been proposed here? How can Christian leaders and communities start a "revolution" of love, grace and mercy? How could we all begin to spend more time on what matters, focusing on the same thing Jesus cares about? The obsession regarding who is saved and who is not is gone when we understand our only calling is to proclaim God's kingdom as an agent of reconciliation. It is not our calling to separate the weeds from the wheat. We let people know who they can become in Jesus, the Son of God. It is their decision to embrace it and take this road or not, to choose love, forgiveness and life, or not.

To close this chapter, I'd like to share what Johnna wrote in our newsletter in April 2016:

Then he said, "Do not come near; take your sandals off your feet, for the place on which you are standing is holy ground" (Exodus 3:5). How many times a day do we take off our shoes in Japan? When we go in someone's home, eat at a Japanese-style restaurant, worship at church, sleep at a cabin, enter a sports locker room, visit a temple, come back home to our house. We take Sophia's shoes off on the train so she can stand on the seat without getting strange looks. For hundreds, probably thousands, of years, Japanese culture (and other Asian cultures) have required the removal of shoes before entering buildings in order to keep dust and dirt off the floor. It makes cleaning so much easier and provides a sense of comfort. Also, removing shoes allows the pressure points in your feet to be stimulated (important for cultures who have practiced reflexology for more than 5,000 years).

Taking our shoes off a lot has made me think of when Moses was approaching the burning bush and God told him to take his sandals off for the "place on which you are standing is holy ground." We see our time here as a time of standing on holy ground. Perhaps years ago it was thought that missionaries went to countries to bring God to the people or to share the story of Jesus for the first time. However, that is not our experience. God made the people we work with in God's image. Jesus has ways of revealing His love and truth that is far beyond the scope of our limited abilities.

So, what is our role? To learn from the people around us, to look for glimpses of God in conversations, to be the hands and feet of Jesus, to observe, listen and act in order to not be obstacles to what God is already doing, but rather instruments of love, mercy, truth and reconciliation.

Chapter 13

Was Jesus a Charlatan?

"I am trying here to prevent anyone saying the really foolish thing that people often say about Him: I'm ready to accept Jesus as a great moral teacher, but I don't accept his claim to be God. That is the one thing we must not say. A man who was merely a man and said the sort of things Jesus said would not be a great moral teacher. He would either be a lunatic — on the level with the man who says he is a poached egg — or else he would be the Devil of Hell. You must make your choice. Either this man was, and is, the Son of God, or else a madman or something worse. You can shut him up for a fool, you can spit at him and kill him as a demon or you can fall at his feet and call him Lord and God, but let us not come with any patronizing nonsense about his being a great human teacher. He has not left that open to us. He did not intend to. We are faced, then, with a frightening alternative. This man we are talking about either was (and is) just what He said or else a lunatic, or something worse. Now it seems to me obvious that He was neither a lunatic nor a fiend: and consequently, however strange or terrifying or unlikely it may seem, I have to accept the view that He was and is God. God has landed on this enemy-occupied world in human form."

C.S. Lewis[62]

---

[62] C.S. Lewis, *Mere Christianity*

To All of Us: Who is Jesus to You?

As we have observed, no matter which culture one comes from, the more we detach Jesus from any religious package, the more we will be provocative and provide a path for people to search and find out about the historical Jesus. If anyone starts reading the Gospel without any clerical interpretation, in honesty and without letting personal or religious trauma to become obstacles in verifying the simple message of Jesus' words, he or she will eventually face the question, "Was Jesus a charlatan?" Was Jesus just someone who was making false claims in order to have a following? Jesus couldn't have been just another light, one of God's many incarnations, just one more master, guru or illuminated human being. He couldn't have been just one more person who has experienced nirvana, no he could not. Either we accept Jesus as who He said He was, embracing his teachings and following him as a disciple, or we choose a different option for our spiritual journey. People are often selective, taking some of Jesus' teachings according to their own interests in order to support their dogmas, religious concepts, philosophical reflections and spiritual journeys. Some people are eager to accept that Jesus was born in Bethlehem, but to believe in his miracles? That's going too far. They admire his teachings and examples given through his beautiful parables, but to believe that Jesus was able to multiply bread and fish, walk on water, quiet a storm, it is too much. It is insane! They may believe Jesus was killed on the cross because the Roman Empire used the cross to show people who was in charge in those days, but resurrection? No, they won't believe it. It is too much to accept.

My response is that we are not allowed to be selective. Following Jesus is the most radical project in life. To follow Jesus is the most fascinating path that any human could take on this earth. If one is following Jesus, if one chooses to be his disciple, there is no room to follow anyone else. If I were to find a word to give us common ground, I would say that Jesus is my philosophical stone. In other words, I read life through Jesus. I read Siddhartha Gautama's (Buddha's) life and teachings through Jesus. I read Confucius, Gandhi, Krishna through Jesus. I read Capitalism, Marxism and all other philosophies of life through Jesus. I listen to the news through Jesus. I observe social and political events through Jesus. What do I mean? That which has to do with Jesus' teachings and spirit according to the Gospels, I say, "well done!" However, that which is not coherent with Jesus' teachings and message, I do not embrace, including some characteristics and ideological thoughts of Christianity as a religious and political phenomenon as mentioned above. The truth is, over time, Jesus has been the object of thousands of psychological, anthropological, sociological, political and religious analyses and countless historical documentaries on TV. Philosophers, writers, poets, psychologists and others have studied His personality. They have discovered that no human being has ever said what Jesus said. His "insanity" began when he was only twelve years old. "When his parents saw him, they were astonished. His mother said to him, 'Son, why have you treated us like this? Your father and I have been anxiously searching for you.' 'Why were you searching for me?' he asked. 'Didn't you know I had to be in my Father's house?' But they did not understand what he was saying to them" (Luke 2:48-50). He went so far as to say, "I and my Father are one" (John 10:30). If he was mentally disturbed, his illness would have been identified immediately. For 2,000 years, no human psychological instruments have been able to detect any type of dysfunction in Jesus' personality. He was always calm, always confident. His "craziness" was always when he was in a lucid state. His "craziness" was sane. Therefore, anyone who reads about his life in the Gospel narratives has the opportunity to make a decision and answer the question for himself or herself, "Who is Jesus?"

One of our most difficult obstacles, unfortunately, has been our religious heritage that we either learned from our family or through Christianity as a religious historical phenomenon, or both. I have not met anyone in recent years who didn't have to work through these two sources. Yet, if someone is able to resolve the trauma of their past, the misunderstanding of Jesus' teachings will fall away and there will be a fascination with Jesus' life and his teachings. The apostle Paul assertively says "in whom are hidden all the treasures of wisdom and knowledge" (Colossians 2:3). In Jesus we have all the treasures of wisdom and knowledge. All! If we want to hear Jesus in His own words, here is what he said to the Jewish people of his time: "'Your father Abraham rejoiced at the thought of seeing my day; he saw it and was glad.' 'You are not yet fifty years old,' they said to him, 'and you have seen Abraham!' 'Very truly I tell you,' Jesus answered, 'before Abraham was born, I am!'" (John 8:56-58). Who else could or would say that? Was Jesus a charlatan? Do we know of any other thinker, philosopher, master or religious figure who has ever made a claim even close to this? Jesus wasn't just another wise "light" in the world. He was radical. He said, "I am THE light of the world. Whoever follows me will never walk in darkness, but will have the light of life" (emphasis mine, John 8:12). Jesus can be our spiritual key to interpret anything in life. Jesus is the fulfillment of the prophecies, he is the expected Messiah, the Christ. He entered the stage of the New Testament and immediately, the Old Covenant was fulfilled, made obsolete, for Jesus is God in flesh and blood.

Can we prove the existence of Jesus?

We have a dilemma before us. How can we scientifically and historically prove Jesus' existence? Do we just trust the narratives? Do we believe Matthew, Mark, Luke and John were telling the truth? Do we assume that Saul was not hallucinating on the road to Damascus? Thankfully, we know there is a difference between scientific proof and legal-historical proof. Josh McDowell discusses this clearly in his famous book, *More Than a Carpenter*.[63] Scientific proof is based on a repeated demonstration in a controlled environment that leads to factual results. For example, if I throw a piece of plastic in water, I see that it floats. If I repeat the procedure over and over again, I will unequivocally conclude that plastic floats in water. On the other hand, I have no way to prove that people existed historically. I cannot prove historical events either. Why not? Because it is impossible to repeat such events and the existence of those people. Why do you and I believe Cleopatra and Napoleon were real people? Why do we believe that Sumerians existed as part of ancient civilization in Mesopotamia more than 3,000 years ago? How do we begin to prove the existence of powerful empires and political systems such as Roman, Greek, Babylonian, etc.? If we go out for coffee today, how would you prove to someone else that you talked to me? In thirty years, how can you prove to your friends that

---

[63] *More than a Carpenter by Josh McDowell*, Tyndale House Publishers, Inc.

we met and talked about globalization and how the world has become so small because of it? Well, in all of these cases, you will prove them through legal-historical proof, not scientific proof.

First, in the case of our in-person conversation, you would immediately become the first witness of this historical event. Next month or next year, you'll remember that we got together and had a conversation. Second, other people who were part of our conversation or saw us talking to each other would be witnesses. Finally, if you or someone else nearby took notes of our conversation, we would have enough proof to show people in thirty years that we met and talked to each other thirty years prior. So, how do we know Jesus really existed? How do we prove the resurrection was real and not a scam? How do we know if Jesus was who he said he was and not a fake? Eleven of Jesus' apostles were martyred for believing that he was who he said he was and that he was resurrected. Only one, John, was not martyred. After those early days, thousands and thousands of followers of Jesus were killed and eaten by lions in Roman gladiator theaters as "entertainment" put on by emperors and other people of power. Did thousands of followers of Jesus die because they believed a lie? Was Jesus, if a con man, able to deceive all of them? Did they accept a fallacy and waste their time, energy and very lives for nothing?

Actually, they were eyewitnesses to Jesus and his resurrection. They walked with Jesus. They testified about who he was and more than that, they testified to who he claimed to be. They participated in his life directly. They transmitted his message orally. They wrote letters concerning historical events, Jesus' death and resurrection. The second and third generations after the apostles who walked with Jesus continued to write thousands of documents about those first historical events. They ratified the message and life of Jesus. Known as the Early Church Fathers, they include Polycarp of Smyrna (c. 69 - c. 155), Clement of Rome (1st Century, traditionally 99 or 101), Irenaeus (early 2nd Century, c. AD 202), Athanasius of Alexandria (c. 293 - 373), among others. If Jesus was mentally ill, his acts would have been without control, selfish and narcissist. Yet, it was the opposite. What we read about is his care for the other, unconditional love and serenity. We are not able to detect insanity or any form of mental illness in his attitudes and behavior. After all, what can we learn from Jesus' life? Which principles can be applied for us today? If Jesus was real, what was his purpose in life?

I read something once by Dietrich Bonhoeffer, the German martyr who was killed by the Nazi regime, in Portuguese. It said something like "the human being has lost the capacity to be human." He was right. It is in Jesus, the Son of Man, the Son of God, that I learn how to be a human being. It is through him that I learn how to interpret life and teach my orthodoxy and orthopraxis to walk together on the same road. No one today will be able to prove if what Jesus said was true or not until he or she can put their feet on the journey of faith. It seems we often forget that Jesus is not competing with any religious figure nor any religion, period. Not Muhammad, Confucius, Krishna, Gautama Buddha or any name you might be thinking of. Christianity, as a religion, might be competing with all of them, but not Jesus. In fact, no religious figures, thinkers, gurus or philosophers have said what Jesus said, therefore, I reach no conclusion other than to affirm that Jesus was and is unique and exclusive. All others become relative to Jesus.

Why do we believe in Jesus? Why do we accept the resurrection as fact? Why do we feel certain that he is alive today? How do we personally discern that he wasn't a fake? I try to put myself in 1st Century culture as I read the Gospels. I imagine reading Paul, Peter and John's letters as if they were personal letters to me. I imagine myself as part of the group that got together at each other's houses to read and listen to the apostles' messages and exhortations. Then, I go a step deeper and try to put myself in the multitude who saw Jesus on the cross. I close my eyes, go back 2,000 years and imagine him right in front of me. For instance, I take the event where Jesus multiplied bread and fish and imagine that I was there. I picture myself as an eyewitness to Jesus' resurrection, one who heard and saw him. I sometimes imagine what it would be like to have been one of his twelve apostles. At the least, I try to imagine what it would have been like to be in the second or third generations after the apostles. I put myself in Egypt or other important areas in the 1st or 2nd Century, imagining life before the Bible existed. What would it have been like to read those first writings, first-hand copies of the apostle's letters? Or at that time, the main form of communication was oral, so what would it have been like to listen to someone telling me about a man named Jesus who came to Jerusalem, did miracles, taught about love and mercy, used parables, claimed he was God incarnate, was misunderstood by his brothers, Jewish people, religious groups, then was killed in the most horrible and shameful way, on a cross, as if he were a murderer? Then imagine that some people said he was resurrected from the dead while others said he even appeared to them after a few days, they saw him alive, they touched him, they watched him eat. Some said they saw this: He was taken up and a cloud received Him out of their sight. And while they looked steadfastly toward heaven as He went up, behold, two men stood by them in white apparel and said, "Men of Galilee, why do you stand gazing up into heaven? This same Jesus, who was taken up from you into heaven, will so come in like manner as you saw Him go into heaven" (Acts 1:9-11, NKJV).

I understand why Luther wrote the famous words, "Preach [and live] as if Jesus was crucified yesterday, rose from the dead today, and is returning tomorrow."[64] In fact, this is my energy and hope today; this is the reason I live and continue to walk this spiritual journey. The cross of Jesus is still fresh before my eyes. I can see it today. My sins have been forgiven. Though Jesus' death on the cross took place long ago, it may feel like yesterday. And today, I celebrate his resurrection. He is alive! Today, I live his life in me, but I am also thankful and believe tomorrow is the day of His return. In short, I live life with expectation and joy, hope and serenity, confidence and peace because He is coming. It is not a coincidence that Paul includes himself and others of his time in the second coming of Jesus. Our brother Paul, full of hope, beautifully writes, "After that, we who are still alive and are left will be caught up together with them in the clouds to meet the Lord in the air. And so we will be with the Lord forever" (1 Thessalonians 4:17).

Leap of Faith Moment

Why do we still have debates about Jesus' existence? When will we take a leap of faith and follow him? It is interesting how many talks I

---

[64] *A Trip around the Sun: Turning Your Everyday Life into the Adventure of a Lifetime* by Mark Batterson, Richard Foth, Susanna Foth, 2015 published by Baker books.

have with people about Jesus as a historical figure. I could write countless historical arguments to justify the historicity of Jesus. You and I could have endless theological debates, putting Jesus next to any guru or religious figure, comparing their teachings and talking about it for hours. However, there is a moment when the arguments end, the theological discussions are put aside, and our attempts at using logic to convince someone that Jesus is God incarnate will be in vain unless God's revelation comes to open someone's mind and understanding. From that point forward, the person is invited to take a leap of faith like Indiana Jones in The Last Crusade. Do you remember the scene where Harrison Ford takes a step off a cliff into empty air and suddenly, a bridge begins to form beneath his feet, allowing him to cross to the other side?

How can we apply this reflection to our missiological goals? How do we talk to people in a way that shows them our devotion to and love for God? How do we demonstrate that what we live out is not "fanaticism, hallucination or imagination", but a lifestyle that is based on emulating Jesus' life and teachings? When we meet people with resistance toward talking about religious matters, God, faith, Jesus, etc., we have the opportunity to deconstruct the common obstacles to historical Christianity. In other words, there is often a negative cloud of Western religion and several possible traumatic religious experiences that most people have due to bad past experiences with their own families or religious groups. In addition, in a country like Japan, much resistance comes from the fact that Japanese people associate me with a Western religion - they see it as something completely other, part of my culture, not as something that might have a direct implication for their own life.

Quick Overview of the Gospels (Matthew, Mark, Luke, John)

So, how do we meet this resistance? Through the Gospels. It is the only way. God may be revealed through nature, God's extrinsic voice. God may be revealed through our conscience, God's intrinsic voice. But it is through the narratives about the life of Jesus that we discover who he truly is. In Mark, we see Jesus as a servant. Mark was a disciple of Peter. Chronologically, Mark was the first written

Gospel, written to a non-Jewish audience. Mark focused his Gospel on Gentiles and Romans. It is no coincidence that we do not see Jesus' genealogy included here. It would not make sense to Gentiles and Romans to have a long introduction of Hebrew characters that were not significant outside of Jewish history. It was unnecessary to bring up any Jewish heritage or traditions because the listeners were not Jewish.

On the other hand, Matthew was writing to a Jewish audience. Therefore, he included Jesus' genealogy. He evokes historical Jewish information and states that Jesus Christ is the Christ of God. He includes stories of Isaiah, Jeremiah, Ezekiel and other prophets who prophesied the coming of Christ in the Old Testament. Matthew highlights that Jesus was the Messiah of Israel and frequently refers to him as the Son of David. Next, the book of Luke. A doctor, evangelist and disciple of Paul, he also wrote the book of Acts. Luke painted the most historical picture of Jesus, including precise chronological events with lots of detail. His Gospel is considered a well researched historical document and he used eyewitnesses to build his narratives. Presented to a Jewish and non-Jewish audience, he describes Jesus' humanity and uses titles such as Christ and the Son of Man.

Finally, the last Gospel, the book of John. This is the most theological of the Gospels. The easiest to read, we see Jesus described as the Word of God, God incarnate, God in the flesh, the divine Son of God. Unlike the other three narratives, John does not include any parables. Rather, it contains seven miracles, thus, it is known as the book of the seven signs. During the Protestant Reformation, all were encouraged to read John due to its simplicity in being understood. I also encourage anyone I meet who has no background on the historical Jesus to read the book of John. I agree with the reformers - we do not need any mediator between humans and the Scriptures. There are no bridges needed between God and humans - no popes, cardinals, pontificates - Jesus bridges the gap. I read the Gospels and find Jesus. I read the Gospels and decide who Jesus is to me personally and what that means for my life.

With this in mind, as we start navigating the Gospels, we will be brought face to face with Jesus. We will see who he is in his own words and then decide who he is to me. No one before or after Jesus said, "I will not leave you as orphans; I will come to you. Before long, the world will not see me anymore, but you will see me. Because I live, you also will live. On that day you will realize that I am in my Father, and you are in me, and I am in you" (John 14:18-20). No one before or after Jesus said they would be in someone's life to give them power, but Jesus said, "But you will receive power when the Holy Spirit comes on you; and you will be my witnesses in Jerusalem, and in all Judea and Samaria, and to the ends of the earth" (Acts 1:8).

No one else has ever said, "I am in you." The idea is Jesus is in us, he lives in us, he dwells in us. It is not a force or a light. It is not an energy or a philosophical comprehension. He literally means he will come and live in anyone who claims his name and follows his teachings. How do we bring up Jesus in our conversations with others? How do we share our spiritual journey in different cultures? How do we live life simply as disciples of Jesus when we are constantly facing different points of views? How can we cultivate opportunities to share our journey as disciples of Christ in our own culture and around the world?

The answer is in and through love. It's as simple as that…

Chapter 14

Do I Have to Evoke Jewish History to Announce Jesus?

"To the Jews I became like a Jew, to win the Jews. To those under the law I became like one under the law (though I myself am not under the law), so as to win those under the law. To those not having the law I became like one not having the law (though I am not free from God's law but am under Christ's law), so as to win those not having the law. To the weak I became weak, to win the weak. I have become all things to all people so that by all possible means I might save some."
The Apostle Paul (1 Corinthians 9:20-22)

For Bible Worshippers Part Two (be sure to read to the end)

If I were in the middle of a forest reaching out to an "unreachable" tribe, or traveling through a small village in the middle of nowhere, and I know no one there has heard of the Bible or Jesus or church, do you think it is necessary for me to bring up historical Jewish events? Is it imperative that I bring up Jewish historical events to people in Papua New Guinea? A small village in Bangladesh? Nomad communities or country tribes in Mongolia, Kazakhstan or Uzbekistan?

I have been observing how confused Christians seem when the topic is Israel. We have become Judaizers over time, without even knowing it. With study of Galatians and Hebrews, we realize that Jesus alone is enough. It is not Jesus and Moses, Jesus and Joshua, Jesus and the prophets. It is not even Jesus and Abraham. It is Jesus… and nothing else. It is not my goal here to go in depth on this topic, but it is a relevant topic to mention when we are discussing a missiological glimpse into any era, culture or people group. Our call is to present Jesus and his message - the good news. Our call is to announce and spread Jesus' name and the story of his life, compassion, love, mercy and hospitality to all. We are to be facilitators and proclaim to the world how Jesus responded to the needy and the poor and forgiving sins. More than that, we are to confirm the message of the apostles, the cross and the empty grave. Jesus was resurrected from the dead and is alive.

There is no need, after announcing who Jesus was to a non-Jewish audience, to go back 4,000 years in history to talk about Moses, the laws, and what happened in Egypt with Israel. For anyone who comes from a Judeo-Christian culture, it is easy to reflect on Jewish history from a Western point of view. It does not require much effort to reflect on God's mysterious ways to reveal Himself to each person on earth if we imagine the culture has the same comprehension as we do of Jewish history. We could spend hours, weeks, even months or years with any group of people on any part of the globe, going through every prophecy in the Old Testament and bringing up all major events in Jewish history, including the major and minor prophets. But what does all that mean to a non-Jewish culture? Jesus said, "'Love the Lord your God with all your heart and with all your soul and with all your mind.' This is the first and greatest commandment. And the second is like it: 'Love your neighbor as yourself.' All the Law and the Prophets hang on these two commandments" (Matthew 22:37-40). What else is more important than love? What else is needed beyond the principles of Jesus in the Sermon on the Mount in Matthew 5? Aren't these principles clear and simple for any person, civilization or tribe?

"Blessed are the poor in spirit, for theirs is the kingdom of heaven. Blessed are those who mourn, for they shall be comforted. Blessed are the meek, for they shall inherit the earth. Blessed are those who hunger and thirst for righteousness, for they shall be filled. Blessed are the merciful, for they shall obtain mercy. Blessed are the pure in heart, for they shall see God. Blessed are the peacemakers, for they shall be called sons of God" (Matthew 5:3-9). Answer me sincerely, what type of person is going to see God? Who are called sons of God? Only the Presbyterians and Calvinists? They didn't even exist when Jesus was preaching this sermon! Only Protestants and Evangelicals? The Protestant movement is only 500 years old and the Evangelical movement is less. Only Pentecostal groups who believe in the power of the Holy Spirit? These movements are not even two hundred years old. Only people who go to buildings with a cross on top? No, not at all!

Recently I was speaking to a person who is a Christian and the question came up, "Fábio, but aren't you going to teach the Old Testament and Jewish history to your daughter?" Of course I will. I love the Old Testament and have studied it since I was nine years old. I am currently in the middle of *The Antiquities* by Flavius Josephus. Hopefully I will finish it in a few more months. I love reading the Old Testament and seeing how God manifested His presence through Jewish history. However, our minds are limited when we think that the world and people of all eras have had access to what we have in our hands. We make a mistake in assuming that every person has received the same Christian and Jewish influences as we have.

For instance, I have never started a conversation about Leviticus. Could you imagine if I were to start with Leviticus, the book of sacrifices and laws, when talking to someone who has not been exposed to the historical Jesus, such as the average Japanese person? Could you imagine if I began conversations with my Sri Lankan friends like this: "During the time of Judges, when there was a famine, an Israelite family from Bethlehem - Elimelech, his wife Naomi, and their sons Mahlon and Chilion - emigrated to the nearby country of Moab. Elimelech died, and the sons married two Moabite women: Mahlon married Ruth and Chilion married Orpah." Be honest with me and let me know if you would start talking about Ruth if you had the chance to visit one of our 240 tribes of Brazilian Indians in the heart of the Amazon rainforest. These tribes represent almost 900,000 people.[65] How can we learn from the apostles? What does Acts teach us? If we take a global perspective covering the civilizations of every era, what would we come up with regarding God's mission and the way to reach every person? When we observe the examples of the apostles, we are able to learn a few principles. Based on their audience, the apostles would change their speech. Today, we should understand how important it is for us to realize with whom we are talking: a globally minded person? Someone who cares a lot about history? A group of people who know the Bible well? A culture with Jewish background? One who has never heard of the minor prophets? Could you imagine how crazy it would be for me to talk to Brazilian Indians in the Amazon about the Jewish minor prophets? I'm pushing you as I like to push everyone to look outside our theological boxes. Please do not misunderstand me. The truth is we are so accustomed to think about evangelism through Western parameters, we forget that not everyone in every culture is bombarded by Christian songs, holidays, books and speakers.

Jewish History For a Jewish Audience

Paul, Peter and Stephen brought up Jewish history and connected it to Jesus when they spoke to Jewish audiences in Acts. Of course, the audience was Jewish! Jesus himself was Jewish. He was the fulfillment of countless prophecies in Scripture. However, we see that when the same apostles spoke to either Gentiles or pagans who didn't have the same knowledge of Jewish customs, they did not bring up any background about Israel. What does this have to do with our missiological glimpse? How can we apply these principles in a practical way when we talk to someone who comes from a Western Judeo-Christian background and someone who does not? Are we given any guidance as to the difference between the two approaches in the book of Acts?

Let's look at Acts chapter 2. In Peter's sermon after Pentecost, he was speaking to people living in Jerusalem, a Jewish audience. He brought up Joel's prophecy saying the Spirit of the Lord would be

---

[65] "Brazilian Indians" at http://www.survivalinternational.org/tribes/brazilian

poured out on all people. Then, he spoke about David to show that God made Jesus, whom they crucified, both Lord and Messiah. At the end of his sermon, after everything else, he said that those who accepted his message would be baptized. As a result of this message, around three thousand were baptized that day. In Acts 7, we see something similar in Stephen's speech to the Sanhedrin. He started his speech with God appearing to Abraham and promising that he and his descendants would possess the land even though he had no children. (The listeners knew Abraham had received the miracle of Isaac). Then, he went on to share about Isaac's son, Jacob, then Joseph and the Pharaoh, then Moses and finally, he was able to connect Jesus to the Eternal Christ. He shared Moses' prophecy to the Israelites, "God will raise up for you a prophet like me from your own people." He was able to keep going in the same direction with the goal of showing them that Jesus Christ was the Christ of God, the promised Messiah.

Peter and John were going up to the temple for prayer, in Acts 3:13-22, when Peter heals a lame beggar. Next, we find one of the most brilliant pearls to understanding Jesus as the hermeneutic key in order to comprehend the Scriptures. Jesus is bigger than any prophet or person who preceded Him. Peter says, "The God of Abraham, Isaac and Jacob, the God of our fathers, has glorified his servant Jesus. You handed him over to be killed, and you disowned him before Pilate, though he had decided to let him go. You disowned the Holy and Righteous One and asked that a murderer be released to you. You killed the author of life, but God raised him from the dead." Have you seen this before? It amazes me because I cannot find a stronger statement about a person anywhere. The Author of Life! No one calls Moses this. No one says this about any of the Old Testament prophets. I don't remember a reference like this when talking about David or Joshua. It is about Jesus - only Jesus, the Author of Life! Peter continues, "We are witnesses of this. By faith in the name of Jesus, this man whom you see and know was made strong. It is Jesus' name and the faith that comes through him that has completely healed him, as you can all see. "Now, fellow Israelites, I know that you acted in ignorance, as did your leaders. But this is how God fulfilled what he had foretold through all the prophets, saying that his Messiah would suffer" (Acts 3:15b-18).

Once again, we see how Peter takes the Jewish historical road to lead the listening audience through all the prophets and Scriptures. Finally, he concludes by saying, "Repent, then, and turn to God, so that your sins may be wiped out, that times of refreshing may come from the Lord, and that he may send the Messiah, who has been appointed for you - even Jesus. Heaven must receive him until the time comes for God to restore everything, as he promised long ago through his holy prophets. For Moses said, 'The Lord your God will raise up for you a prophet like me from among your own people; you must listen to everything he tells you'" (Acts 3:19-22a). I like that. Peter is urging us, "You must listen to everything he tells you," (Acts 3:22b). Who is the "he" that Peter is talking about? It is clearly Jesus, the One Moses said God would raise up like a prophet among them. Moses said he would be bigger than Moses and that the Jewish people who were used to having prophets, were supposed to listen to him.

Jesus also brought up historical facts and prophecies from Scripture to remind Jewish audiences what had been said about him. On the road to Emmaus, Jesus said to the two men, "How foolish you are, and how slow to believe all that the prophets have spoken! Did not the Messiah have to suffer these things and then enter his glory?" (Luke 24:25-26). Then, he reminds them what Moses and the prophets said about him.

Apostle Paul - Man of Discernment Who Knew His Audience

How about Paul? Do we have examples of him changing his speech to match his audience? When he is speaking to a Jewish crowd, he brings up the history of Israel, but when not, he does not. In Acts 13, Paul and Barnabas went to Pisidian Antioch. One Sabbath, after reading from the Law and the Prophets, the leaders of the synagogue said, "Brothers, if you have a word of exhortation for the people, please speak" (Acts 13:15b). Then Paul stands up and talks about how God made the people prosper when they were in Egypt. He tells of how Canaan was given to the people as their inheritance. He continues talking about judges, Samuel, Saul, David and finally, how from David's descendants, "God has brought to Israel the Savior Jesus, as He promised" (Acts 13:23b).

I'm impressed that Paul's speech has a beginning, middle and end. It fascinates me to see that he knew what to say to whom and how to talk about different scenarios depending on the listeners. "The people of Jerusalem and their rulers did not recognize Jesus, yet in condemning him they fulfilled the words of the prophets that are read every Sabbath" (Acts 13:27). Have you noticed before that the leaders of the synagogue read and read about the Messiah, memorizing the text, reading the prophecies every Sabbath, and yet were unable to understand the fulfillment of God's promises? The speech ending says that Jesus was executed on the cross and after being taken from the cross and laid in a tomb, God raised him from the dead. For many days he was seen by those who had traveled with him from Galilee to Jerusalem.

Paul took them down this well-known historical road and then said, "We tell you the good news: What God promised our ancestors he has fulfilled for us, their children, by raising up Jesus. As it is written in the second Psalm: You are my son; today I have become your father. God raised him from the dead so that he will never be subject to decay. As God has said, "I will give you the holy and sure blessings promised to David. So it is also stated elsewhere: 'You will not let your holy one see decay.'" Now when David had served God's purpose in his own generation, he fell asleep; he was buried with his ancestors and his body decayed. But the one whom God raised from the dead did not see decay. "Therefore, my friends, I want you to know that through Jesus the forgiveness of sins is proclaimed to you. Through him everyone who believes is set free from every sin, a justification you were not able to obtain under the law of Moses" (Acts 13:32-39). Once again, how could the leaders read and read about the Messiah every Sabbath and not see God's fulfillment of promises in Jesus?

There is just one reason. If God doesn't reveal Himself to a person, he or she can read the Scriptures day and night, but will still have the veil over their eyes. How about a non-Jewish culture? How about Paul when he's before a non-Jewish audience? Is there anything in Acts that tells us it is crucial to bring up Jewish history to a non-Jewish culture? In Acts 17:16-31, Paul is talking to a group of non-Jewish people in Athens, at the Areopagus. He does not bring up any Jewish history. His audience has nothing to do with Exodus, Leviticus, Moses and laws, Jericho, temples in Jerusalem, David or anything else related to Israel. Why didn't he bring up anything related to Jewish tradition or evoke the prophecies that were fulfilled in Jesus? Because they obviously weren't relevant in that context. The Greeks were not familiar with Jewish history, therefore, Paul spoke about the historical background of the city, even quoting philosopher Epimenides, to create a bridge or common ground and lead naturally into telling about Jesus.

Athens had a horrible plague and many people died. The elders believed there was a type of curse on Athens and so they tried offering sacrifices to all of their gods, but nothing happened. After that, Epimenides, who knew how to appease the offended god, said that there was an unknown God who was great and good, he would stop the plague if they invoked his help. They prayed to the unknown God and finally, the plague stopped. Then, Paul stood during the meeting with Areopagus and said, "People of Athens! I see that in every way you are very religious. For as I walked around and looked carefully at your objects of worship, I even found an altar with this inscription: to an unknown god. So you are ignorant of the very thing you worship—and this is what I am going to proclaim to you..." He continued saying: "The God who made the world and everything in it is the Lord of heaven and earth and does not live in temples built by human hands. And he is not served by human hands, as if he needed anything. Rather, he himself gives everyone life and breath and everything else. From one man he made all the nations, that they should inhabit the whole earth; and he marked out their appointed times in history and the boundaries of their lands. God did this so that they would seek him and perhaps reach out for him and find him, though he is not far from any one of us..."

Next, Paul referred to Greek philosopher, Epimenides: "As some of your own poets have said, 'We are his offspring.' Therefore since we are God's offspring, we should not think that the divine being is like gold or silver or stone—an image made by human design and skill. In the past God overlooked such ignorance, but now he commands all people everywhere to repent. For he has set a day when he will judge the world with justice by the man he has appointed. He has given proof of this to everyone by raising him from the dead."

Why isn't it considered essential to bring up Moses, the prophets, David and Old Testament laws when I talk of Jesus with a group of non-Jewish people who have a totally different context than Western society? Well, what do the laws of Moses have to do with Jesus and the good news? Do we see the world through American-Judeo-Christian lenses? As mentioned before, the Bible can be the mother of all heresies, a knife in the hands of a drunkard, if Jesus is not my key to interpret the Scriptures.

Since I was nine, I have been learning how to interpret the Scriptures. I have learned how important it is to consider the cultural biblical context, the historical background, the political situations behind the text, the primitive mentality of people 3,000 years ago, the importance of the meaning of any word in one of the original Biblical languages (Aramaic, Greek or Hebrew). I have learned to compare diverse translations, understanding 1st Century and B.C. contexts. For example, the importance of studying rabbis Hillel and Shammai to understand what Jesus meant when he talked about divorce, or studying the backgrounds of Isaiah, Jeremiah, Luke and Paul to better understand their prophecies and writings. But more important than all this is to interpret the Scriptures through Jesus' life and words because he is our main hermeneutic key to understanding the message of Scripture.

"Where is it Written?" (Please, Covenanters, do not get me wrong)

It is important to ask, "Where is it written?" as long as Jesus is the hermeneutic key. In the past, Moses ordered the stoning and killing of false prophets (Deuteronomy 5). Jesus, however, just said to be careful about prophets, to watch and discern: "Beware of false prophets, who come to you in sheep's clothing, but inwardly they are ravenous wolves. You will know them by their fruits" (Matthew 7:15-16). Psalm 137 is also a good example. In the beginning of the Psalm, there is a nostalgic sense of longing for Zion in a foreign land. We see what some may consider to be a worshipping of the sacred place of Jerusalem. But Jesus shows us worship is not about a sacred location: "But the hour is coming, and now is, when the true worshipers will worship the Father in spirit and truth; for the Father is seeking such to worship Him. God is Spirit, and those who worship Him must worship in spirit and truth" (John 4:23-24). In

Jesus, true worship is not about being on Mount Gerizim or in Jerusalem, but it is about the true and sacred geography of our hearts - with sincerity and honesty in spirit and in truth. Still in Psalm 137, "Remember, Lord, what the Edomites did on the day Jerusalem fell. 'Tear it down,' they cried, 'tear it down to its foundations!' Daughter Babylon, doomed to destruction, happy is the one who repays you according to what you have done to us. Happy is the one who seizes your infants and dashes them against the rocks" (Psalm 137:7-9). By contrast, when John, James and Jesus entered a certain Samaritan village, Luke reveals how Jesus should be my hermeneutic key to interpret the Scriptures and life. "When the disciples James and John saw this, they asked, 'Lord, do you want us to call fire down from heaven to destroy them?' But Jesus turned and rebuked them. Then he and his disciples went to another village" (Luke 9:54-56). When I put these two texts and several other texts from the Old Testament next to Jesus' teachings, I am able to compare how obsolete and primitive was the mentality and spirituality of a person three thousand years ago to our current awareness of human rights and social justice, but, especially compared to Jesus's teaching who very often tells me "You have heard that it was said to those of old...But I say to you...."

It is God's word from the mouth of the Living Word of God compared to God's words in a certain time or circumstance, to a certain cultural or spiritual perspective with partial understanding and shallow comprehension used as archetypes and hints for what would come. So, not just "Where is it written?", but also, "What is written?" My reflection does not need to be limited to a 21st Century Western-Judeo-Christian culture lens. God is infinitely bigger than Western society and Christian heritage - American, Evangelical, Protestant, Orthodox and Catholic points of view.

Once again, in how many countries is it forbidden to read or study Scripture? In how many cultures and political regimes are people punished for speaking Scripture? Millions of people, from past to present, have never heard or read a single verse from any of the Scriptures. Was God confined to a book? Was God unable to speak to those cultures and civilizations in other ways? How did they ever hear about Jesus? How could they have ever discerned who God is if no church, missionary or Christian organization had reached them in the distant regions of the globe? How did they ever experience God's salvation if no one was allowed to speak freely about the historical Christ? If we think back to before the Protestant Reformation, before the 16th Century when the Bible was only read by Catholic priests, popes, scholars and bishops - how was God speaking to the rest of the millions of people, tribes and inaccessible villages?

My reflection has a presupposition about all humans from every era and culture in history. Everyone has access to God's Living Word. In other words, if we were to find a message like, "Honor your parents and take care of your children and family" in any Aztec writings on a wall in a cave, those instructions are God's words because they are coherent with the spirit of the Gospel and the Living Word of God, Jesus. If we were to find a concept about forgiving your enemy in any Sumerian stone writings or writings on rocks left by an indigenous tribe, we would know they are God's words. In these cases, it doesn't matter where it is written, but what is written because it shows us how "every good and perfect gift is from above, and comes down from the Father of lights, with whom there is no variation or shadow of turning" (James 1:17).

I am shocked when I hear Christians justifying aggressive behavior, unfair wars, the death penalty, any brutal human action by quoting a few Old Testament texts and interpretations without considering the context. There was a complete primitive spirituality 4,000 or even 2,000 years ago - a relative and limited mentality among barbarian[66] civilizations in a different era. Are we disciples of Elijah or Jesus? How can we reconcile Elijah, Moses, David and Jesus? We cannot! I do not want David as my example, do you? I do not want Moses as my example, do you? I do not want Elijah as my example, do you? James says, "Elijah was a human being, even as we are," (James 5:17a). Those men walked their journey, made decisions by faith, some good, some bad and through it all, they offered a sincere heart to God. Today, they are examples to us, but in

---

[66] I recognize that this term is outdated and no longer accepted in anthropological circles. In *Evolutionism In Cultural Anthropology: A Critical History*, Chapter 8, Developmental Stages, states: "...the words savage and barbarian grew too jarring to the increasingly sensitive anthropological ears." They reference The Berndts (1973:20) who stated a case for no longer using these terms.

Jesus I find what I need to pursue who I should become. When I was sixteen years old, I was already starting to realize that Christians are so confused, diverging as an evangelical moment, trying to conciliate Jesus and Moses, the New and Old Testament, the God of the Old and New testament, etc. If it is confusing for those who are claiming to be disciples of Jesus, can you imagine how confusing it is to those are in a completely different cultural context? Can you imagine trying to explain and merge a message from 3,000 years ago with Jesus' good news to non-Christian and Jewish nations if they have not received any of our cultural influences? As we talk honestly to people and get to know them and their cultures, travel experiences, observe their idiosyncrasies, learn their religious backgrounds and see they have a totally different historical influence than our Judeo-Christian heritage, we will be able to see that the historical Jesus is all they need. The apostle Paul said, "Christ is the culmination of the law so that there may be righteousness for everyone who believes" (Romans 10:4). Christ is the culmination. He is the end. He is the fulfillment of the law!

Jesus "having canceled the charge of our legal indebtedness that stood against us and condemned us; he has taken it away, nailing it to the cross" (Colossians 2:14). When we read in Matthew 5:18, "For truly I tell you, until heaven and earth disappear, not the smallest letter, not the least stroke of a pen, will by any means disappear from the Law until everything is accomplished," we notice the verse that completes the puzzle is on the cross when Jesus said, "It is finished," (John 19:30). The Greek word, τετέλεσται (tetelestai), means that literally, it is finished! As an instrument of salvation, the law died. Otherwise, we would say what Paul says in Galatians 2:21, that "if righteousness comes from the law, then Christ died in vain." The law makes us feel guilty, it increases the condemnation in us. The reason is simple, it is because the law is good and holy and I am not. Galatians and Romans confront this tension clearly and directly. If I wanted to be saved by observing the law, I would have to obey every single part of it, the entire package. That is what James, the half brother of Jesus teaches: "For whoever keeps the whole law and yet stumbles at just one point is guilty of breaking all of it" (James 2:10). Therefore, if we fail in 1% of the law, we are already unqualified to be saved by the law. Who has never coveted? No one escapes this one simple commandment.

The law before Christ was like a tutor, guiding me and showing me my imperfections, proving that I couldn't be saved by human effort. Paul says in Galatians 3:24-26, "So the law was our guardian until Christ came that we might be justified by faith. Now that this faith has come, we are no longer under a guardian." The law shows me I cannot be saved by it. The more guilty I feel, the more I transgress. This is a cycle that we see played out in any addiction program where life stories reveal that repression exacerbates the addiction and the forbidden makes the temptation much bigger than it is; fear turns into invincible monsters and ghosts. If we were only able to be saved through the law, by keeping all of it, obeying it in all aspects, spheres and categories, we might have a chance on an objective level. But, when we add the subjective sphere as well, no one is able to do it. No one is innocent regarding the subjectivity of the law. Even if I do not commit adultery as a fact, if I have lust in my heart, I am already guilty for Jesus says, "But I tell you that anyone who looks at a woman lustfully has already committed adultery with her in his heart" (Matthew 5:28). I may not have wooden or golden idols, but if I covet gold from a temple, I have already failed. I may not have human-made idols, but if I crave a successful career that I build in my own image, I have already failed. I may not take the name of God in vain, but if I declare war, have prejudice and justify these things on behalf of God, producing separations and walls between social classes, races and cultures, I have already taken the name of the Lord in vain. Therefore, not one of us is able to observe and obey 100% of the law as an instrument of salvation. The law died on the cross.

What are we to do if no one is able to survive such condemnation? What are we to do if we are not able to follow the law and please God? We look upon Jesus, the pioneer and perfecter of our faith, to be justified. Paul says, "For it is by grace you have been saved, through faith - and this not from yourselves, it is the gift of God" (Ephesians 2:8) and "Therefore, since we have been justified through faith, we have peace with God through our Lord Jesus Christ," (Romans 5:1). Where else did the law die? Where else can we see Jesus as the fulfillment of God's promises and past archetypes in order to allow us to see how the law was part of a past primitive mentality? For example, the ceremonial laws also died: Passover, the laws in the tabernacle, the temple, the burning of sacrifices. Jesus is the fulfillment of the ceremonial laws. Jesus is the Lamb of God, the Temple, the Sacrifice, the meaning of Passover.

Obviously, the moral laws in any society need to be preserved. The social laws of the Decalogue (the Ten Commandments) are present in nearly all civilizations around the world. They might not have phrases like, "Love God above all else," but almost all countries base their legislation on common laws such as you shall not murder, you shall not steal, etc. The Ten Commandments are the minimum for any society to be reasonable and fair with rules that create good and safe social cohesion. Paul goes further in Galatians 5:22-23, "But the fruit of the Spirit is love, joy, peace, forbearance, kindness, goodness, faithfulness, gentleness and self-control. Against such things there is no law." Against such things there is no law? What is he talking about? The answer is very simple. The only law in Jesus is love - whoever loves does not take the name of God in vain. Whoever loves keeps not just the Sabbath, but every day holy in order to serve his or her neighbor. It becomes not just a break from work, but every day is an opportunity to devote her or himself to God. Whoever loves does not commit adultery, honors his father and mother, doesn't lie, doesn't steal. Love is the only "law" that when followed, covers all the social laws. A person who loves obeys the other laws without even realizing it.

We cannot forget what Isaiah says, "All of us have become like one who is unclean, and all our righteous acts are like filthy rags; we all shrivel up like a leaf, and like the wind our sins sweep us away" (Isaiah 54:6) Only in Jesus do we find our cover - tetelestai - it is finished! If love is there, there is an awareness of my neighbor's needs. If love is there, there is an awareness of myself, my social environment and everything else related to life. In love, through the fruit of the Spirit, we find out that "against such things there is no law." This is the message you and I are invited to proclaim to every nation, culture and people group that have or have not received Judeo-Christian influences: "You shall love the Lord your God with all your heart, with all your soul, with all your mind, and with all your strength. This is the first commandment. And the second, like it, is this: You shall love your neighbor as yourself. There is no other commandment greater than these" (Mark 12:29-31).

Chapter 15

The Order of Melchizedek

"I revealed myself to those who did not ask for me; I was found by those who did not seek me. To a nation that did not call on my name, I said, 'Here am I, here am I.'"
Isaiah 65:1

Melchizedek - A Mysterious Character

Here we begin what is, in my opinion, one of the most fascinating and mysterious topics in the Bible. In fact, I never heard about Melchizedek when I was growing up, but my mentor taught me how important it is to see the connection between him and Jesus. This topic was my mentor's thesis when he was ordained a pastor in 1977 in Brazil and since then, it has been part of his teaching for decades. Since I first heard it from him, I began talking, studying and reflecting on Melchizedek, king of Salem, priest of the Most High God, and Jesus who comes from the order of Melchizedek. Most of us have read the verses in Genesis and Hebrews that mention Melchizedek, but have not spent much time reflecting on them to go deeper in interpretation. Have you ever heard of the connection between Melchizedek and Jesus?

Perhaps you have read Don Richardson's *Eternity in Their Hearts* and remember when he brings up the Melchizedek factor. The order of Melchizedek, however, goes even farther and provokes each of us to reflect on something that may change our basic view of how God's amazing love, perfect plan of salvation, mysterious ways, Sovereignty and freedom to behave as God have been present since the beginning of the world. He has been pursuing humankind through a unilateral initiative that we read about in Genesis when God came and asked Adam, "Where are you?" (Genesis 3:9). "The Lord said to Abram: "Get out of your country, from your family and from your father's house, to a land that I will show you. I will make you a great nation; I will bless you and make your name great; and you shall be a blessing. I will bless those who bless you, and I will curse him who curses you; and in you all the families of the earth shall be blessed" (Genesis 12:1-3, NKJV). Also in Genesis, we learn that Abram has a father, comes from the city of Ur of the Chaldeans, has a family background and hears God's voice to leave his country to be a blessing and part of a nation. Abram was called to make God's name great and all the families of the earth be blessed.

What can we observe by following Abram's journey? What was God's main purpose in calling Abram? God revealed Himself to Abram who later became Abraham. As we study Abraham's journey, we see he is part of a tribe that became a nation responsible to carry the message that there is One God, One Creator of the Universe. The same nation became Israel, which was responsible to register God's Word, the Scriptures, and be the historical source of God's revelation on earth. In Genesis 14, we see that after Abraham returned from war, a mysterious character named Melchizedek (king of Salem, king of peace) showed up. Melchizedek brought out bread and wine - he was the priest of the God Most High. He blessed Abram saying, "Blessed be Abram of God Most High, Possessor of heaven and earth; And blessed be God Most High, who has delivered your enemies into your hand" (Genesis 14:18-20).

Melchizedek is introduced to us as the priest of the God Most High. Wasn't Abraham also priest of the God Most High? Wasn't Abraham chosen by God to carry His revelation? How could Melchizedek also be a priest of the God Most High? Did Abraham tell Melchizedek about God? How is it that Abraham gave Melchizedek his tithe? Wasn't Abraham superior to Melchizedek? God is not confined. Abraham didn't tell Melchizedek about God.

God revealed Himself to Abraham, but could also reveal Himself to other people without Abraham's permission. God, indeed, disclosed Himself to Melchizedek. When we observe Melchizedek bringing out bread and wine, we see the representation of communion thousands of years before Jesus would establish what we call today our historical sacrament of faith. Melchizedek didn't have a father, genealogy or historical connection; the only thing we know about him is the fact that he knew God.

Before continuing, I'd like to ask you to keep the text of Genesis 14:18-20 in mind and also observe a few texts in Hebrews that are about Melchizedek which give a new layer of comprehension of the Genesis passage. Hebrews 6:20 mentions the entrance of the forerunner, Jesus, the one who became the High Priest forever, in the order of Melchizedek. What grabs my attention is the fact that Jesus didn't come from the tribe of Levi, but of Judah. He is compared to Melchizedek who was said to have neither beginning of days nor end of life, therefore, he was timeless. The author of Hebrews constructed this analogy since Jesus is the forever High Priest.

Hebrews 10:5-7 is simple and self-explanatory. "Therefore, when Christ came into the world, he said: "Sacrifice and offering you did not desire, but a body you prepared for me; with burnt offerings and sin offerings you were not pleased. Then I said, 'Here I am - it is written about me in the scroll - I have come to do your will, my God." Continuing in verses 9-14: "Then he said, 'Here I am, I have come to do your will.' He sets aside the first to establish the second. And by that will, we have been made holy through the sacrifice of the body of Jesus Christ once and for all. Day after day every priest stands and performs his religious duties; again and again he offers the same sacrifices, which can never take away sins. But when this priest had offered for all time one sacrifice for sins, he sat down at the right hand of God…For by one sacrifice he has made perfect forever those who are being made holy."

The order of the Levites was definitely a temporary priesthood made by mortal men who offered sacrifices from time to time, repeating the same sacrifices and never having the ability to take away sins. Yet Jesus, offered for all a single sacrifice for sins - the body of Jesus Christ, once and for all. I love the analogy between the shadow and the real form that projects the shadow. The law, the temporary priesthood, the sacrifices, every religious ritual, were simple shadows of the real figure that is Jesus. Therefore, they all became obsolete in the presence of the one who projected the shadow. We observe two ways God reveals Himself to humankind. 1) The historical revelation that comes from Abraham who had a genealogy, father, mother, culture, ethnicity - in other words, he is someone we are able to track down. We also see historical elements of God's people in the Bible because they are descendants of Abraham. 2) God's eternal revelation through Melchizedek. It is through him that we discern that God can reveal Himself at any time, in any way, to any person in any culture. Abraham has a beginning and an end. We know his name, last name, genealogies, historical events, families and more. However, in Melchizedek, God shows up without any human permission or approval. We see His absolute freedom to be God. Can you imagine if God had only revealed Himself through Abraham's descendants? Can you imagine if all civilizations depended exclusively on Abraham's descendants to know God's historical information? Can you imagine if God's voice came only from the priesthood class?

God would be limited, boxed into a social, cultural and religious instrumentality. We read in the Old Testament that there were constant conflicts and tensions between the priesthood class and the prophets. On one side, the priesthood class (the Levites) was the representative of God. It was theoretically the "only way" God could manifest his presence. On the other side, we had the prophets claiming that God could manifest His will and presence through and with the Levites, but also in spite of them and without them. Here's the Hebrews text that points us back to Genesis, "For this Melchizedek, king of Salem, priest of the Most High God, who met Abraham returning from the slaughter of the kings and blessed him, to whom also Abraham gave a tenth part of all, first being translated "king of righteousness," and then also king of Salem, meaning "king of peace," without father, without mother, without genealogy, having neither beginning of days nor end of life, but made like the Son of God, remains a priest continually. Now consider how great this man was, to whom even the patriarch Abraham gave a tenth of the spoils. And indeed those who are of the sons of Levi, who receive the priesthood, have a commandment to receive tithes from the people according to the law, that is, from their brethren, though they have come from the loins of Abraham; but he whose genealogy is not derived from them received tithes from Abraham and blessed him who had the promises. Now beyond all contradiction the lesser is blessed by the better. Here mortal men receive tithes, but there he receives them, of whom it is witnessed that he lives. Even Levi, who receives tithes, paid tithes through Abraham, so to speak, for he was still in the loins of his father when Melchizedek met him. Therefore, if perfection were through the Levitical priesthood (for under it the people received the law), what further need was there that another priest should rise according to the order of Melchizedek, and not be called according to the order of Aaron? For the priesthood being changed, of necessity there is also a change of the law" (Hebrews 7:1-12).

Abraham Face to Face with Melchizedek

In summary, we find in Abraham a certain faith that is seen and touchable. Without Abraham, we would not have Israel or Jerusalem. It is because of Abraham that we study and discover a faith that has formed history and a certain people and culture that are visible and related to God. On the other hand, no one will say that it is because of Melchizedek that we have a certain people or culture. Because we do not, Melchizedek is mysterious. We are unable to see a list of his descendants or understand where he came from or what happened after him. It is not visible, but rather an inexplicable way to see how God has infinite ways to manifest Himself outside of human control. We cannot understand this relationship between God and Melchizedek. How was God revealed to Melchizedek? In a dream? A vision? Through a historical event, personal experience, something else? We are encouraged to reflect here and see how God has a parallel way that doesn't use Abraham, therefore, all of us today see God has a parallel way that does not require a pastor, church, missionary, rabbi, liturgical process, priest or ceremony. It is the beauty of understanding the power of Missio Dei. Mission of God means it is done by God, using his angels and his freedom to speak to whomever he wishes. In Abraham, we find a book, a land, pedigree, border, and even a theology.

On the other hand, Melchizedek is a way that is exclusive to God, an absolute mystery similar to the incarnation that allows Jesus to be both fully human and fully define. I walk in the historical path of Abraham and his journey. It is how I am able to discern God in history. I have access to the Scriptures and can see God's progressive revelation of Jesus through the Scriptures and the convergence with God's people as part of Abraham's descendants. We have received God's revelation through historical channels, but we do not know where and to whom God is revealing His face right now. Some people are uncomfortable with this because they want to have the certainty of knowing what God is doing in the world at all times. However, God is God and has the right to be so, without needing our permission or approval to fulfill his mission.

It is in Melchizedek that we may find God's fingerprints anywhere as we walk through life on this existential path. Sometimes we will realize that God has already arrived at a certain place, culture or people group before us because God is God and is free to do whatever God wants. We learn not to be arrogant or presumptuous by thinking that God is only able to work and speak to the world through us. When Jesus said, "I am the way, the truth, and the life. No one comes to the Father except through Me" (John 14:6), he is not implying, "No one comes to Jesus except through 'us'" (as in you and me helping Jesus).

People have been receiving glimpses of God's revelation for centuries. I have often asked myself what will happen to civilizations where the stories of Abraham, Isaac, Jacob, and even Jesus, have not been told. If we presume that God is free and that Missio Dei does not depend on us to be accomplished, what then is our role? Are we really responsible to proclaim the Gospel? If we quit sending people to places that have never heard of the historical Jesus, could we just rely on God because we know He will find a way to reveal Himself to those people? No! We absolutely should take responsibility to go and preach the good news, be agents of reconciliation, proclaim that "God was reconciling the world to himself in Christ, not counting people's sins against them. And he has committed to us the message of reconciliation" (2 Corinthians 5:19).

It is our responsibility and we cannot transfer it to someone else. It is our call to understand and embrace the Great Commission. However, we are not called to establish the final judgment and separate the wheat from the chaff. We are not called to assume that we are God's only representatives on earth. We are not called to believe that God cannot do anything without us, thinking we are the only way to manifest God's salvation in the world. We are called to be humble enough to affirm that God is God and free to speak to "Melchizedeks" anywhere. Wherever we cannot reach out, God is able. Wherever there are tribes and groups of people that we do not know of, God knows. Our human tendency and religious temptation is to think we know everything God is doing, but we do not.

We follow Abraham's footprints, but then we learn that Jesus belongs to a superior order, that of Melchizedek. In Abraham, we have the historical Jesus; in Melchizedek, we have the Eternal Christ. Jesus comes from Abraham, but belongs to Melchizedek. He is the Savior of those who know his name, and also of those who do not. He is the one who works on people and cultures that know his name while also working on those people and cultures who do not. We belong to the faith that comes from Abraham, from the historical promise and God's blessing that embraced each one of us. "For when God made a promise to Abraham, because He could swear by no one greater, He swore by Himself, saying, 'Surely blessing I will bless you, and multiplying I will multiply you'" (Hebrews 6:13-14, NKJV). Later, in Hebrews 7:12, we find out one of the most precious verses related to Jesus, His priesthood, the old covenant and the law. "For when the priesthood is changed, the law must be changed also" (Hebrews 7:12). When we declare that we follow Jesus, it means we belong to a new order, a change in the law. We do not belong to the order of Levi, the order of religion, because the law died in Christ. Hallelujah! There are no more rites or sacrifices. Jesus is everything we need. In Christ, the law died and at the same time, was fulfilled, because the law ultimately never made anyone perfect. In contrast, Jesus makes us perfect through his perfect sacrifice. We are justified by him. He belongs to the infinitely superior order of Melchizedek. "For such a High Priest was fitting for us, who is holy, harmless, undefiled, separate from sinners, and has become higher than the heavens; who does not need daily, as those high priests, to offer up sacrifices, first for His own sins and then for the sins of the people, for this He did once for all when He offered up Himself" (Hebrews 7:26-27). It was necessary to change the law. It is a higher priesthood, not from the order of Levi, but from the order of Melchizedek, that puts me face-to-face with God's freedom and makes me bow down before His sovereignty.

Chapter 16

An "Angel" on my Path

I say to you that many will come from the east and the west, and will take their
places at the feast with Abraham, Isaac and Jacob in the kingdom of heaven.
Jesus (Matthew 8:11)

And My Writings Became a Book...

It is near the end of our journey. When I told Johnna I would write a
few ideas down before talking to her missions professor, Paul De
Neui, I never expected that it would turn into pages and pages of my
reflections and thoughts. During this time, Johnna often came to me
and asked if my writings were ready. "Not yet, please give me a few
more days." Then, I realized I had written more than fifty pages. One
day, when writing our newsletter in Spanish for Project Japan, I
accidentally saved our newsletter over this document, erasing about
thirty pages. Yes, I did! So, what you have been reading is not
exactly the original document. When I realized what I had done, I
started trembling and couldn't believe I had lost so much. I texted
Johnna and said, "Johnna, you're not going to believe this, but I was
about to finish the last two chapters of my reflections and after three
months of daily writings, suddenly everything is gone." Or so I
thought. The good news is I had done a backup about ten days before

my mistake, so I could rescue a good portion of the original. However, it took me a while to find the courage to come back and redo dozens of lost pages. I almost gave up.

What was the learning process? Why didn't I give up? What made me think, "I can do it!"? What made me move past my mistake and start anew? What made me think it would be worth it to persevere? Well, I found the comfort and encouragement needed by realizing I live in Japan - a culture that has taught me how to rebuild things from scratch, how to persevere in spite of everything, how to be thankful and never give up, how to think positively and how to move on. I was able to take a deep breath and restart the final chapters in order to make it to the end.

One morning, Johnna went to work and I stayed home to watch Sophia the entire day. We had been working on Sophia's routine, adjusting her bedtime so she would skip her afternoon nap and get tired and go to bed between 7 and 7:30pm. It was dinnertime. Sophia and I went grocery shopping. I decided not to bring her stroller because I didn't want her to fall asleep on the way to the store. But as soon as we got to the store, Sophia asked me to put her in one of the grocery carts for kids. She loves those carts and they make grocery shopping much easier. Well, what I wasn't expecting was that she might fall asleep. I saw her eyes slowly shutting and as I gave my credit card to the cashier, I said, "Sophia, don't fall asleep! Daddy is going to make dinner for us." But it was too late. I didn't have her stroller and I had to carry four grocery bags home by myself. She was totally passed out. I realized she would skip dinner and wake up hungry in the middle of the night… and I would have to explain to Johnna that our brilliant idea to adjust Sophia's routine was making things worse.

I had to do something. So, I did. I decided to walk back home, telling myself I could make it with four bags of groceries and a two and a half year old in my arms. I reminded myself of the many times I had traveled around the world with huge suitcases and guitar cases. I started walking the fifteen minute journey back home. In the beginning, it wasn't so difficult though I had to be careful because Sophia's head was bouncing from side to side. As I walked, Sophia's body kept getting heavier and heavier. I reminded myself I could do it, "Go, Fábio! Go, Fábio! You can make it. Keep going. Just a little more…" It was dark and I could barely see the people on the street. I thought, "I have only about five minutes left, but it's going to take me twenty minutes if I keep walking at this pace. I'm not going to make it…"

As I was getting ready to put Sophia on the ground to rearrange the bags, I felt two hands on my shoulders. Two different women were touching me. One was a young woman, about thirty-three years old. The other was a bit older. They saw me carrying Sophia and realized the desperateness of my situation. They didn't know each other, but they came to help me at the same time. I immediately started talking to the older lady as I also thanked the younger lady by bowing my head many times and smoothly saying, "Arigatou gozaimasu." (Thank you very much!). Well, I don't know how she understood my basic Japanese, but the older woman helped me. She ended up carrying my groceries and walking me back home. She put my groceries on the balcony in front of our door and I was able to prepare Sophia's bed and put her in it. Tears wet my eyes as I concluded that an angel had helped me get back home safely with Sophia. I wish I could express my gratitude to that Japanese woman in better words. Honestly, I could tell you multiple stories and experiences like this that I have had since I moved to Japan. The values here are love, respect, sincerity, transparency, generosity, altruism, collective thought instead of an individualistic way to live life.

What does this have to do with our glimpse of missiological experiences? In a country where the number of Christians is so low, how do we answer questions regarding heaven and hell, evangelism and churches? How do we reconcile these low numbers with our Christian concept that if they are not Christians and not attending evangelical churches, they are ultimately not saved and are not going to heaven? I was probably about twelve years old when for the first time, I heard a local pastor answering a question about heaven and hell. As you might imagine, a person had passed away who was not considered a "Christian", didn't attend our church, belonged to a different religion, and so you can guess what kind of answer our teenage Sunday School class received from our professor. But the truth in these situations is we do not have these answers. When I'm asked about people's destiny, my sincere and honest answer is, "I am not the secretary of the Holy Trinity, therefore, I do not know." Yes, hell exists. Yes, hell is real. Yes, Jesus talks about a place that we have come to understand as hell. But also, yes, Christianity has done a horrible work in this area by not bringing up the "good news" and instead, giving a message based on fear throughout many generations convincing millions of people that if they do not attend church and become Christians, their destiny will be hell.

Let's Pause Here

I do not intend to go much deeper on this matter. Otherwise, I would probably write a hundred more pages. But, I do have a few questions. Do you know that out of 7 billion people, only about 2.2 billion are Christians in the world today?[67] Where will the other 4.8 billion people go? Is there an easy answer? Can we possibly split heaven and hell between Christians and non-Christians? Is this how God sees his created beings, his children made in his image? What about hundreds and thousands of years ago when Christianity was less popular than today? There are about 49 countries with a Muslim majority.[68] Most of the world's Muslim population lives in Africa and South Asia, particularly Indonesia, Pakistan and India.[69] With their high number of atheist citizens, China and Hong Kong appear to be outliers in Asia.[70] Buddhism has almost 500 million followers,

---

[67] "8" percent of the world population has faith; a third are Christian" by Jennifer Harper, The Washington Times at http://www.washingtontimes.com/blog/watercooler/2012/dec/23/84-percent-world-population-has-faith-third-are-ch/

[68] "Muslim-Majority Countries" at http://www.pewforum.org/2011/01/27/future-of-the-global-muslim-population-muslim-majority/

[69] "The Future of the Global Muslim Population" on http://www.pewforum.org/2011/01/27/the-future-of-the-global-muslim-population/

[70] "Map: These are the world's least religious countries" at https://www.washingtonpost.com/news/worldviews/wp/2015/04/14/map-these-are-the-worlds-least-religious-countries/?utm_term=.86f6293d71ce

representing 7-8% of the world's total population.[71] Hinduism has over one billion followers representing about 15% of the world's population.[72] Most live in India, Nepal, Bangladesh, Indonesia, Pakistan and Sri Lanka.[73] An estimated 160 million people live without access to any Scripture in their heart language. 1.5 billion people have only partial access to Scripture in their first language. Even with over 2,422 worldwide active projects, translation work still needs to be done in a remaining 1,800 languages, according to the Wycliffe Association.[74]

Historically speaking, Christianity has generally changed the good news of Jesus into a type of "fire insurance" message saying, "Come to Christ so you can avoid going to hell." We quickly see the polarized dilemma when we look at the Universalist view on the other side of this fire insurance. God is love, so therefore, hell does not exist and everyone is destined to live with God forever. We must find the balance. Hell is real, but God has no pleasure in sending someone there. Hell is real, but it was prepared for Satan and his angels. "Then, He will say to those on his left, 'Depart from me, you who are cursed, into the eternal fire prepared for the devil and his angels'" (Matthew 25:41). Hell is real and everyone who wants to go there will go and continue their selfish, egocentric, narcissistic life. Hell is real and much bigger than a transcendental experience for we know millions of people have been living in existential hell for years. Hell is real and Jesus talked about it, comparing it to the Valley of Hinnom near Jerusalem (also called "Gehenna"), a huge

[71] "Buddhists" at http://www.pewforum.org/2012/12/18/global-religious-landscape-buddhist/

[72] "The Global Religious Landscape" at http://www.pewforum.org/2012/12/18/global-religious-landscape-exec/

[73] "Top Ten Countries with Largest Hindu Population" at http://www.mapsofworld.com/world-top-ten/world-top-ten-countries-with-largest-hindu-populations-map.html

[74] "What's been done, What's left to do" at https://www.wycliffe.org.uk/wycliffe/about/statistics.html

garbage dump where dead bodies and trash burn day and night in continuous fires. However, he spoke about it to a very specific audience - the religious group that was filled with hypocrisy, insincerity, pseudo-knowledge and cult of personality. He says, "You are of your father the devil, and the desires of your father you want to do. He was a murderer from the beginning, and does not stand in the truth, because there is no truth in him. When he speaks a lie, he speaks from his own resources, for he is a liar and the father of it" (John 8:44).

Hell - Delicate and Controversial

Hell is real and Jesus was clear in his message. "Woe to you, scribes and Pharisees, hypocrites! For you travel land and sea to win one proselyte, and when he is won, you make him twice as much a son of hell as yourselves" (Matthew 23:15). Hell is real, but it will have an end. "Then death and Hades were thrown into the lake of fire. The lake of fire is the second death" (Revelation 20:14). I personally cannot picture a medieval understanding of a bunch of people being tortured and burned, while on the other side there are "saints" saying something like, "You did not hear us, you did not come to our churches, you didn't join our Bible studies, you didn't raise your hands and accept Jesus into your hearts. We told you this would happen..." Next to that group, we might picture a sarcastic god looking at those who are saved and those who are burning forever. This is much more a picture of an evil god than of a God of love and grace. If that image has anything to do with any god, that god is probably Satan, not our merciful God. Unfortunately, the strongest image humans have of hell was built in the middle ages based on Inferno, the concept as described in Dante Alighieri's 14th Century poem, *The Divine Comedy*. The more I observe God's unilateral initiative, unspeakable love, freedom to be God at work in any culture at any time before anyone even has access to the historical information of Jesus, the more I understand what Paul says concerning the secrets of people's hearts. "For when Gentiles, who do not have the law, by nature do the things in the law, these, although not having the law, are a law to themselves, who show the work of the law written in their hearts, their conscience also bearing witness, and between themselves their thoughts accusing or else excusing them in the day when God will judge the secrets of men by Jesus Christ, according to my gospel" (Romans 2:14-16). The more I keep studying text after text in the Scriptures about how we cannot define God, understand His ways fully or confine Him to a systematic theological view, the more I understand Jesus' words when He says:

"When the Son of Man comes in this glory, and all the angels with him, he will sit on his glorious throne. All the nations will be gathered before Him, and He will separate the people one from another as a shepherd separates the sheep from the goats. Then the king will say to those at his right hand, 'Come, you that are blessed by my Father, inherit the kingdom prepared for you from the foundation of the world; for I was hungry and you gave me food, I was thirsty and you gave me something to drink, I was a stranger and you welcomed me, I was naked and you gave me clothing, I was sick and you took care of me, I was in prison and you visited me.' Then the righteous will answer him, 'Lord, when was it that we saw you hungry and gave you food, or thirsty and gave you something to drink? And when was it that we saw you a stranger and welcomed you, or naked and gave you clothing? And when was it that we saw you sick or in prison and visited you?' And the king will answer them, 'Truly I tell you, just as you did it to one of the least of these who are members of my family, you did it to me'" (Matthew 25:31-40).

I love to read that Jesus is gathering all the nations. I can even picture people coming to him, nation by nation. The truth is Jesus has never used categories to separate people: Christian vs. non-Christian, Protestant vs. Catholic, Evangelical vs. non-Evangelical. Rather, he always uses concepts like children of the light, children of the darkness, those who listen to his commands and put them into practice vs. those who do not practice them, those who love vs. those who do not love. When it comes to people who know or do not know his historical name, we see that people in both categories have come to know him and follow him in some way. "O the depth of the riches and wisdom and knowledge of God! How unsearchable are his judgments and how inscrutable his ways! For who has known the mind of the Lord? Or who has been his counselor? Or who has given a gift to him, to receive a gift in return? For from him and through him and to him are all things. To him be the glory forever. Amen" (Romans 11:33-36).

Many people have heard and learned about Jesus and then received God's revelation to follow the Eternal Christ of God who is Jesus of Nazareth, the Son of God. It is also true that many, many people have received God's revelation through a dream, vision or divinely inspired event, then later learned about Jesus and decided to follow him. Many who have not heard of Jesus eventually receive God's revelation, practice His will, follow the Eternal Christ of God without knowing he is Jesus, and they will be there on that final day. They did not know Jesus' name, but they knew his commandments to love one another. They chose life. They might be shocked when they meet Jesus face to face saying, "I thought you came from a Western religion. I thought you were absolutely different. Were you the same Jesus they proclaimed when they came to our land carrying swords and crosses, raping our women, robbing our wood and gold? When did we meet you? I was one of the only survivors among my indigenous tribe in Central America."

Or a nomad group of men may say, "Where have we met you? We were nomads in the 11th Century and lived in a place that is called Azerbaijan today. We heard of Christians and Muslims killing each other on behalf of "god." They mentioned a man named Jesus, but we wanted nothing to do with those lands, conquerors, beliefs and ideologies. We lived our lives in simplicity with love and compassion."

Or a man who lived during the 6th Century in a village that is now in Cambodia or Laos may say, "I didn't even know you were born in Bethlehem and grew up in Nazareth. I had no idea. We had no Bible, missionary or church! When did I meet you, Jesus?"

There will be just one answer, "You met me when you met the one who was hungry and you gave him a piece of bread, you met me when you raised your voice against social injustices and embraced those refugees, you met me when you were able to forgive the chief from a different tribe who came and killed your women and children. You met me when you embraced the cause of immigrants and marginalized individuals. You met me when you met those orphans in the terrible civil war in Syria. You met me when you met the widow. You met me when you visited those lonely elders. You met me when you heard the voice and practiced hospitality with love and care to the man who walked the streets in the Bronx with a gold medal on his chest, looking like a strong young man, but depressed and without hope. You thought you embraced him, but you were embracing me. You met me when you met the one who was thirsty and naked and you came to meet his needs. I was there. I was one of them."

I Have a Question For You!

My question is this: Have you seen Jesus recently? Have you seen him over there, next to you? In your neighborhood? In your family? As you travel and walk the streets? As you ride the bus or stop at a traffic light? When the Omega Day comes, we will understand that we only knew everything in part. We had only a glimpse, a poor, superficial, shallow understanding of the great and indescribably amazing love of God. We will find out that many people who confessed the name of Jesus also carried in their heart prejudice against social class and skin color, thoughts of supremacy and megalomaniac goals, homophobia, building walls instead of bridges and acting out in racism and hate. They could have chosen to do good, but they did not. More than that, they strained out gnats while swallowing camels not realizing that little by little, they began walking the abyss to become people who had nothing to do with the Kingdom of Love. It is like those who passed the Good Samaritan in the gospel of Luke. Were they too busy? Late for something important? Didn't these religious people know the Scriptures? The Law? How God instructed us to care for the poor and marginalized? Weren't love and compassion important words in their liturgies? "Then, Jesus will say to those on his left, 'Depart from me. I was hungry and you gave me nothing to eat, I was thirsty and you gave me nothing to drink, I was a stranger and you did not invite me in, I needed clothes and you did not clothe me, I was sick and in prison and you did not look after me.' They also will answer, 'Lord, when did we see you hungry or thirsty or a stranger or needing clothes or sick or in prison, and did not help you?'"

"We knew your historical name, we read your parables, we memorized countless psalms, sang in choirs with gregorian chants, attended monasteries, temples, seminaries, and conferences." Sadly,

Jesus will reply, "Truly I tell you, whatever you did not do for one of the least of these, you did not do for me." And more than that, Jesus will say to them "I never knew you. Get away from me, you who practice evil!" We will probably find out that we were wrong in our theological certainties and we wasted time by playing politics on behalf of religious convictions. We will also see how many times we went through meaningless theological debates only to realize in the end, we would finally know as we have been fully known by the Only One able to know hearts and minds fully because he made each of us in his image to become like him.

I would like to invite the late John Stott to help me finish this controversial and delicate subject. John Stott summarizes what we learn about God from His promise to Abraham and its fulfillment. In John Stott's article, "He is the God of mercy," it says "I have always derived much comfort from the statement of Revelation 7:9 that the company of the redeemed in heaven will be "a great multitude which no man could number." I do not profess to know how this can be, since Christians have always seemed to be a rather small minority, but Scripture states it for our comfort. Although no biblical Christian can be a Universalist (believing that all mankind will ultimately be saved), since Scripture teaches the awful reality and eternity of hell, a biblical Christian can - even must - assert that the redeemed will somehow be an international throng so immense as to be countless. For God's promise is going to be fulfilled, and Abraham's seed is going to be as innumerable as the dust of the earth, the stars of the sky and the sand on the seashore."[75]

With that in mind, I remember what I learned from a friend of mine recently. He said I will probably have three surprises when I am face-to-face with the Light, Jesus, the Eternal Christ of God. The first surprise will be those who are not there. I will be looking for some folks who I thought were supposed to be there, but where are they? They were always talking about God, prophesying, getting into theological and apologetic arguments, carrying their Bibles under their arms, trying to impose their "divine experiences" on everyone they met in São Paulo, Barcelona, Toronto. They even did wonders

---

[75] The living God is a Missionary God, John Stott (page 9) Perspectives on the World Christian Movement edited by Ralph D. Winter and Steven C. Hawthorne

in the name of Jesus in front of thousands and thousands of people. They used stages, stadiums and theaters as pulpits and platforms to preach, they spoke on the radio and on TV. What happened? I thought they would be here, but they are not...

The second surprise will be those who are there that I never thought would be there. I will say, "What?! How is this possible? What are they doing here? Look at that man, I remember him. He was in the bar almost every day in Barcelona. He did not stop drinking. Look at that woman. No way!! She used to work in the Red Light District in Amsterdam. She is here! I never imagined they would be here, but here they are. I cannot understand how this happened."

After the two surprises, I will think at that moment, "Today, I finally and fully understand the simple and clear message of Jesus when He alerted us: 'Not everyone who says to me, 'Lord, Lord,' will enter the kingdom of heaven, but only the one who does the will of my Father who is in heaven'" (Matthew 7:21). I will also understand what Jesus meant when he spoke against the spirit of hypocrisy and pharisaism. "Truly, I say to you, the tax collectors and the prostitutes go into the kingdom of God before you" (Matthew 21:31).

And the final and biggest surprise will be even more shocking than the first two. I will look at myself and say: Wait a minute! I am here. I am here, too…

I will look at myself, touch my arms, hands and head, surprised, and replete with joy, I will say I am here by God's amazing grace. I am here, saved by Jesus, not for what I have done or who I am, but because of His extravagant love, forgiveness, and sacrifice on the cross. I am here, not by my own virtue, but because of what He has done and because of who He IS.

Made in the USA
Middletown, DE
24 May 2018